God Is My Witness

Making a Case for Biblical Divorce

By Cindy Burrell

God is My Witness

Unless otherwise noted, Scripture references are from the
New American Standard Version.

Library of Congress Cataloging-in-Publication Data
Burrell, Cindy
    God Is My Witness: Making a Case for Biblical Divorce

Printed in the United States of America, Lulu Press
ISBN# 978-1-312-679603

Published by Cindy Burrell, Hurtbylove.com
Original © 2009 by Cindy Burrell, All Rights Reserved
www.hurtbylove.com

Editing assistance provided by Charla Woods

Cover design provided by Corey Michael,
thecoreymichael@yahoo.com

New American Standard 1995 Bible version used for
reference unless otherwise noted.

Dedicated to those who listen to one small voice above all others.

Let those who love the Lord hate evil, for He guards the lives of his faithful ones and delivers them from the hand of the wicked.
Psalm 97:10

Table of Contents

God Is My Witness

Foreword

This book has been written for those who doubt, for those who are not content or perhaps even afraid to move forward without knowing that the ground upon which they are standing is solid and sure. This is for those of you have questions about what you have been told, what you have read, what the experts say, whether divorce is a sin and whether you are at risk of being abandoned by God. Although these things are broadly taught, there are aspects of those teachings which are undeniably contrary to the very nature and heart of God.

So you come seeking answers. You are searching for the truth.

This book is for you. My intent in writing this book is to enable the reader to look beyond all of the religiosity, church-iosity, legalism, and common misappropriations of Scripture in order to find the heart of our almost unperceivably merciful Father-God, whose heart overflows with grace and truth and power and provision all wrapped up in His love of relationship - with you.

Do not fear, for when your heart is open and pure toward Him, He will meet you and hold you and show you how perfect His heart is.

This may not be an easy journey. Although the truth you find in these pages may give you peace and comfort, and your relationship with your Lord may deepen, others in the faith community, family and friends may not accept the freedom God grants you. Many have even left the family of faith because of the judgment and rejection to which they have been subject.

Nevertheless, the truth will set you free.

"Those who come to God must believe that He is, and that He is a rewarder of them that diligently seek Him." Hebrews 11:6

i

Introduction

My shield is with God, who saves the upright in heart. Psalm 7:10

While people may misunderstand me, God cannot. And while others may not see where my heart lies, He does. I take great comfort in that for I will, at times, be misunderstood, misrepresented and misjudged. Yet my shield is with God.

I am a divorcee. For some, that alone provides adequate cause for some to discredit any insight I may have to offer. In truth, such readers are precisely the people who, if I may be so bold, *should* continue reading.

In fact, it is as a direct result of my blemished history, bolstered by my love for the One who has redeemed me, that I have ventured to accept this undertaking. This work began – as with all such works – with a question. What about divorce?

I entered this seemingly dangerous realm, not to justify the road I have traveled, but to more clearly understand it - from God's perspective; for there was without question a moment when the Lord released me from my 20-year marriage bond to my abusive husband. Yet, just as assuredly, even years after, I come across countless columns and commentaries stating without exception or apology that Christian divorce is unacceptable in all circumstances or, in some more lenient texts, is acceptable only if adultery has poisoned the relationship or perhaps in cases of abandonment. So I wonder where I, and others like me, fit in that little box. I have contemplated whether the box was created by God or man. Or, at the other extreme, if perhaps there is no box at all.

There are those within the body of believers who, once informed of my marriage failure, assert a mysterious, almost divine right to know why it occurred. There is often a design to assess the circumstances surrounding the divorce, conjecture as to which of the married partners may have inflicted the most damage, and conclude who is ultimately to blame. Judgment is cursory, and many first-marriage believers seem to believe they hold to a higher rung of righteousness on the ladder of spirituality. And, according to the *letter of the law*, divorce may not be considered adequate to avoid the label of "adulterer" or, in my case "adulteress." In fact, divorce may provoke the label rather than free one from it.

Then why, I wonder, am I free? Why am I not condemned? Why have I sensed God's comfort, His compassion and affirmation? How could I have experienced such a rich peace as my personal Father-God walked with me through every step of my divorce process if what I had done was clearly a violation of His will? How could God release me from my marriage if being released is absolutely contrary to His word? As I have been released, have not others also? What exotic or unexplored piece of this puzzle was missing?

I certainly do not claim to be an exception to any rule or theological truth. So the wholeness of my relationship with God while simultaneously being wholly wrong is inconsistent, if not spiritually impossible. The legalists would assert that I was not supposed to be divorced (or remarried) and still be content, let alone blessed. Certainly, under our common understanding of the *law,* I should be burdened with some measure of conviction.

As I have pored over the Scriptures, searching for a *lawful* explanation for the peace I enjoy, tenets of the law have at times felt incredibly strict, unforgiving, or downright harsh. But, as I have sought God's heart, the Holy Spirit has moved me, not away from the law, but beyond it, and toward the *heart* of God.

Although there are times when we choose the law over love, Jesus did the opposite. He did not nullify the law, He fulfilled it. And our relationship with Him becomes all the law we need. Yet what I have "discovered" is not new at all. The truth radiates through every page, parable and psalm. The discoveries I have made are altogether obvious and simple, yet wondrous. The challenge is to adequately present to the reader the message that we seem to have taken for granted, assumed we have understood, yet so often overlooked. Sometimes we look too narrowly, too deeply, too rigidly and miss the simple beauty that our Creator has set literally right before our eyes.

For while I searched the Scriptures, the Lord enlarged my perspective, taking me far beyond my scope of sight, showing me that the end game is not about the law at all. Nor is it about how people see me; it's about who God is, His design, His intent – His heart. It's all about *relationship*. This life, and my small role in it, comes down to my love for the Lord, and His love for me – and His love for you. It revolves far less around what you or I do and far more around our motives and how the unique personal touch of the Holy Spirit in our lives is manifested.

He alone justifies. He alone sees what lies in my heart. And, while God does not see perfection, He sees who I am and hope to be in Him.

To be forthright, I have actually petitioned the Lord to release me from what I have felt is a calling on my life to write this. I feel inadequate, unworthy and more than a little intimidated by the nature of the subject matter. Yet, I have also sensed His conviction, affirmation and blessing, and therefore I must press on.

My intent is to educate those contemplating divorce or struggling with the judgment that follows. I am also asking those within the contemporary church to tear down and reconsider what has reigned as the traditional church script on the question of biblical divorce, but I am *not* asking the church to ignore or twist what the Scriptures say. Rather, I am asking the church to acknowledge what the Scriptures have said all along.

And I urge patience, dear reader. What is seen with the mind's eye cannot always be simplistically conveyed. Although subtle, contrasting tones can transform a stark, white canvas, there may be moments when it is difficult to see how every hue and shade complements the others until, with a few meticulously laid brush strokes, the intended image emerges.

What follows may not be what you expect. It is not what I expected, either.

So, the journey begins.

But if you are led by the Spirit, you are not under the law.
Galatians 5:18

God Is My Witness

Making a Case for Biblical Divorce

What We Have Been Taught

Divorce is an emotional issue among believers, and each of us comes to the table with preconceived notions of what is acceptable and unacceptable in accordance with the teachings of Scripture. Our tendency is to look at the issue through a narrow lens, with our walls up and our convictions thoroughly entrenched. I confess that, when I accepted this undertaking, my understanding was similarly immoveable.

So before we look deeper at the essence of relationship and take an in-depth biblical look at the issues relating to marriage and divorce, it is appropriate to lay out the church's common teaching on the subject of divorce. Below I have referenced the key Scriptures that are most often cited when discussing the subject, and a brief summary of the basic tenets that these Scriptures are generally believed to support. This is not by any means exhaustive, but is intended to serve as a starting point from which the basic premise may be discussed.

For this reason a man shall leave his father and his mother, and be joined to his wife; and they shall become one flesh. Genesis 2:24

On the occasion of marriage, a man leaves his parental home and a new familial unit is formed that consists of the husband and wife. Once joined in marriage, it is understood that the couple has entered into a one-flesh union which, in God's eyes, is indivisible and inviolable.

When a man takes a wife and marries her, and it happens that she finds no favor in his eyes because he has found some indecency in her, and he writes her a certificate of divorce and puts it in her hand and sends her out from his house, and she leaves his house and goes and becomes another man's wife, and if the latter husband turns against her and writes her a certificate of divorce and puts it in her hand and sends her out of his house, or if the latter husband dies who took her to be his wife, then her former husband who sent her away is not allowed to take her again to be his wife, since she has been defiled; for that is an abomination before the Lord, and you shall not bring sin on the land which the Lord your God gives you as an inheritance. Deuteronomy 24:1-4

If, during the course of the marriage, a woman's husband discovers something lewd, indecent or improper, he may write her a certificate of divorce and send her out of his house. In such a case, the divorced wife may re-marry but may never again return to be her original husband's wife, even in the event of the death of a subsequent spouse. He is also free to re-marry.

"For I hate divorce," says the Lord, the God of Israel... Malachi 2:16a

God is always opposed to divorce. It is an affront and an offense to the One who has joined the two together.

[Jesus said,] "It was said, 'Whoever sends his wife away, let him give her a certificate of divorce'; but I say to you that everyone who divorces his wife, except for the reason of unchastity, makes her commit adultery; and whoever marries a divorced woman commits adultery." Matthew 5:31-32

Even in cases where a writ of divorce is provided, a man who marries a divorced woman forces her to commit adultery and he himself commits adultery.

Some Pharisees came to Jesus, testing Him and asking, "Is it lawful for a man to divorce his wife for any reason at all?" And He answered and said, "Have you not read that He who created them from the beginning made them male and female, and said, 'For this reason a man shall leave his father and mother and be joined to his wife, and the two shall become one flesh'? So they are no longer two, but one flesh. What therefore God has joined together, let no man separate." They said to Him, "Why then did Moses command to give her a certificate of divorce and send her away?" He said to them, "Because of your hardness of heart Moses permitted you to divorce your wives; but from the beginning it has not been this way. And I say to you, whoever divorces his wife, except for immorality, and marries another woman commits adultery." Matthew 19:3-9, Mark 10:2-12

When petitioned by the Pharisees, Jesus made it clear that there was no occasion that permitted divorce. Rather, He reasserted what they already knew: that once married, man and woman constitute one flesh and no man should break the relationship apart. When pressed as to the reason that Moses allowed divorce, Jesus also confirmed that it divorce is an issue that arises out of a hardened heart. Only in cases where adultery occurs is divorce allowed, and if a divorced person remarries under a circumstance other than adultery, they too commit adultery.

But to the married I give instructions, not I, but the Lord, that the wife should not leave her husband (but if she does leave, she must remain unmarried, or else be reconciled to her husband), and that the husband should not divorce his wife. But to the rest I say, not the Lord, that if any brother has a wife who is an unbeliever, and she consents to live with him, he must not divorce her. And a woman who has an unbelieving husband, and he consents to live with her, she must not send her husband away. For the unbelieving husband is sanctified through his wife, and the unbelieving wife is sanctified through her believing husband; for otherwise your children are unclean, but now they are holy. For how do you know, O wife, whether you will save your husband? Or how do you know, O husband, whether you will save your wife? (I Corinthians 7:10-14, 16)

A wife must not leave her husband as long as he is satisfied to have her remain with him. If she does leave him for whatever reason, she must not remarry, but must only reconcile with her husband. Similarly, a husband should not divorce his wife if she consents to remain with him. Even an unbeliever may come to believe as he witnesses the example and faith of his or her spouse. If the unbelieving spouse leaves, once divorced the believing spouse who remains is free to remarry. This is permissible because, in such cases, the married couple is unequally yoked. (II Corinthians 6:14)

Then Peter came and said to Him, "Lord, how often shall my brother sin against me and I forgive him? Up to seven times?" Jesus said to him, "I do not say to you, up to seven times, but up to seventy times seven." Matthew 18:21-22

No matter how many times a brother or sister sins against us, we are obligated to forgive every offense indefinitely according to the directive given by our Lord, assuming that the petition for forgiveness is authentic.

If I speak with the tongues of men and of angels, but do not have love, I have become a noisy gong or a clanging cymbal. If I have the gift of prophecy, and know all mysteries and all knowledge; and if I have all faith, so as to remove mountains, but do not have love, I am nothing. And if I give all my possessions to feed the poor, and if I surrender my body to be burned, but do not have love, it profits me nothing.

Love is patient, love is kind and is not jealous; love does not brag and is not arrogant, does not act unbecomingly; it does not seek its own, is not provoked, does not take into account a wrong suffered, does not rejoice in unrighteousness, but rejoices with the truth; bears all things, believes all things, hopes all things, endures all things.

Love never fails... I Corinthians 13:1-8a
There is nothing that love cannot conquer. Love is a force given to us by God through the Holy Spirit that we can all exert to act

with compassion and sincerity regardless of how we are treated in return, even in marriage. It always focuses on the best in everything, forgives and remains steadfast. In love, we find the strength of character that births positive change. If we truly love, we can endure anything.

Wives, be subject to your own husbands, as to the Lord. For the husband is the head of the wife, as Christ also is the head of the church, He Himself being the Savior of the body. But as the church is subject to Christ, so also the wives ought to be to their husbands in everything. Husbands, love your wives, just as Christ also loved the church and gave Himself up for her, so that He might sanctify her, having cleansed her by the washing of water with the word, that He might present to Himself the church in all her glory, having no spot or wrinkle or any such thing; but that she would be holy and blameless. So husbands ought also to love their own wives as their own bodies. He who loves his own wife loves himself; for no one ever hated his own flesh, but nourishes and cherishes it, just as Christ also does the church, because we are members of His body. For this reason a man shall leave his father and mother and shall be joined to his wife, and the two shall become one flesh. Ephesians 5:23-31

The order of marriage places the husband as the head of the wife just as Christ is the head of the church. The wife's role is to be submissive to her husband just as she is to submit to the Lord. At the same time, the husband is to love his wife as Christ loved the church, having given Himself for her, the husband loving his wife just has he loves his own body, nourishing and cherishing her. In respecting and living according to this example, the one-flesh union will be evident.

In the same way, you wives, be submissive to your own husbands so that even if any of them are disobedient to the word, they may be won without a word by the behavior of their wives, as they observe your chaste and respectful behavior. Your adornment must not be merely external—braiding the hair, and wearing gold jewelry, or putting on dresses, but let it be the hidden person of the heart, with the imperishable quality of a gentle and quiet spirit, which is precious in the sight of God. For in this way in former times the holy women also, who hoped in God, used to adorn themselves, being submissive to their own husbands; just as Sarah obeyed Abraham, calling him lord, and you have become her children if you do what is right without being frightened by any fear. You husbands in the same way, live with your wives in an understanding way, as with someone weaker, since she is a woman; and show her honor as a fellow heir of the grace of life, so that your prayers will not be hindered. I Peter 3:1-7

Wives can also have an impact on the quality of their marriages through their submissive ways and godly behavior. A woman's gentle and respectful manner can most certainly influence the conduct and faith of her husband. A husband is to honor his wife as a weaker vessel, recognizing her as a sister in the Lord. In doing so, he can be certain that his prayers will be heard.

In conclusion, divorce should not be accepted as a common occurrence within the Christian community, yet divorce statistics find that Christians divorce at a rate almost identical to that of unbelievers. This is tragic and demonstrates the hardness of heart in the lives of Christians who have accepted a worldly doctrine that should be wholly unacceptable among people of faith. People in church leadership are also found to be accepting of divorce rather than standing against it for the sake of the ordained institution of marriage, the image of the relationship between Christ and the church, as well as the children affected by the casual acceptance of divorce.

As we make our marriage vows before God in the presence of witnesses, we voluntarily embrace a lifelong commitment to an imperfect person. Though divorce was tolerated in the Old Testament, Jesus makes it plain that God does not approve of the practice, and only in instances of adultery is it to be considered.

Divorce becomes an adulterous act if the divorced person remarries, since Jesus states in Luke 16:18 that, *"...whoever divorces his wife and marries another commits adultery; and whoever marries a divorced woman commits adultery."* The one-flesh union is never really severed in the eyes of God. Divorce and remarriage are, therefore, matters that must be addressed very seriously. For those in Christ, repentance and mutual submission can heal the broken bond.

Forgiveness is available. I John 1:9 reminds us that, *"If we confess our sins, He is faithful to forgive us our sins and to cleanse us from all unrighteousness."* In the Gospel of John, Chapter 8, Jesus forgives the adulterous woman, acknowledging that her sin was no greater or worse than others, Christ knows that we all have sin in our lives. Having been forgiven, she is also nevertheless admonished to *"...Go, and sin no more."*

In cases where a couple is unequally yoked, and the unbeliever leaves and divorces his or her spouse, the believing spouse is free to remarry.

"Yet if the unbelieving one leaves, let him leave; the brother or the sister is not under bondage in such cases, but God has called us to peace." I Corinthians 7:15

This is pretty consistent with what the biblical scholars typically teach. And from many corners of the Christian community, there is nothing left to be said on the matter.

With all humility, I must assert that I have come to disagree that this teaching represents the only, last or most accurate word on the subject. In fact, while the terms are correct, I believe that the order by which we use them, and at times the context from they are taken, is incorrect or at least misunderstood. So we examine not only the law, but the essence of it. For we so often cling to the law, yet fail to embrace what lies behind it. Something far greater, something deep, alive and true.

7

There is the law and there is the love story.

They each reflect the nature of our Father, yet one was the foundation for the other.

There is More to the Story

It could well be said that those doctrines we have largely been taught are based upon several foundational principles and particularly give the impression that 1) there is no marital challenge that cannot be conquered with God's help, precluding the need for divorce in any circumstance; 2) a spouse ultimately possesses power to influence and change the conduct of his or her spouse's faith and behavior; 3) if our spouse fails to change, it is because we lack the faith necessary to bring change about; or 4) our suffering is appropriate, either because we are "doing it wrong," or our suffering is in accordance with the divine will of God.

I believed it all. For 20 years, I lived my married life with all of those Scriptures and promises anchored deep within me. I rested upon a confident assurance that my husband would eventually turn and become the man of God I thought he was when I met him and believed he both wanted to be and could be. Our marriage began well enough, but it wasn't long before there were cracks in our relationship, largely the result of serious lapses of integrity on his part – lies and deceptions, addictions, an unfaithful heart and major controlling tendencies. We still had some good times, and I believed they would eventually outshine the troubles in our relationship. I did my best to fill the role of dutiful wife, prayed for my husband and kept his secrets.

Over the years, I came to live in a fearful state of *"What next?"* I never knew what I might find or be subject to from my husband when I came home or he did. Everything revolved around his moods, wants, desires, and needs. There were periodic discoveries of his battles against an addiction to porn, drugs and alcohol, and I could never seem to do enough to please him, while I was considered selfish if I asked anything of him he did not wish to give.

He emphasized my spiritual failings, telling me that I was unforgiving or not as loving, giving or submissive as a godly wife should be. Yet, similar standards and expectations did not apply to him. On the contrary, I was to trust him without question, even when his behaviors merited questioning, there were blatant signs of overt betrayal or he was overtly cruel and abusive both to me and our children. Any attempt to resolve outstanding issues met with incredulity that I would dare to question or expose him.

We had four children together. As the abuse intensified, my husband and I met with various counselors, and they and my believing friends basically affirmed that, as long as he wasn't hitting me, I had to stay. My husband always had a good story to tell. He rehashed his history growing up in an abusive, dysfunctional home, and periodically arrived at life-changing epiphanies that I believed would yield a genuine faith and a healthy marriage but never gave way to lasting change.

The ups and downs turned into an incremental downward spiral of ever-escalating abuse – verbal and emotional, and it began to take a toll on my physical and emotional health. I suffered from various health issues which included intestinal problems and the onset of various food allergies, which, I have learned since, can be a result of an immune system overcompensating for stress. I struggled with depression, and fear served as the primary emotion that governed our home life.

Although our world became frighteningly unpredictable, I strived to live by all of the biblical principles I had been taught. I believed I could win my husband without a word, that my godly example would inspire him. I held to a confidence that my prayers had the power to touch a hardened heart. I honestly believed that one day our marriage would become all I ever dreamed it could be with the touch and blessing of God. I saw it in my mind's eye - the day when he and I and our kids would stand hand in hand at the edge of eternity whole and happy and full of faith and living in the full richness of the blessing of God.

But it was the faith I thought would save my then-husband that instead empowered and emboldened him. He knew that my relationship with my Lord was the most important thing in my life. He used the very thing I treasured most against me, demanding submission and unconditional love in the name of the God he himself mocked with his lifestyle choices and his treatment of me and our children.

The basic premise under which he operated was that he could treat me any way he wished and, as long as I didn't catch him in the act of adultery, there was nothing I could do about it. I could not leave him nor divorce him, and he made that clear to me. The pastors to whom I spoke and my believing friends basically asserted the same in accordance with the principles of *What We've Been Taught,* leaving me and our children in bondage to a man who professed Christ but was not living as a believer and very clearly preferred his role as dictator and tyrant.

I was not the only one who suffered, as I was to discuss any disagreement with him in private. Only after emotional damage had been inflicted upon our children could I speak to him to petition him for a greater measure of grace and understanding toward them. He would dismiss my petitions under the guise of knowing better than I, and I felt painfully powerless to protect them. Fortunately for them and for me, the day finally came when I found the courage to speak up in the moment, which was not without cost.

It must be understood that it was the traditional church script that gave my former husband the power he sought and exercised to his full advantage. And what my children and I received from him was not love or grace or a godly example; it was terror.

I have come to understand that not only are my former husband's traits and behaviors consistent with those demonstrated by abusers, whether physical, verbal, emotional, sexual or spiritual, they are also consistent with narcissism and even, perhaps, sociopathic tendencies.

Many people of faith would still contend that I had no cause to divorce him, no right or privilege or freedom to do so. With their words and under the doctrine they confess, it would seem that God does not have the authority to intervene or command justice or mercy; that though my former husband broke our marriage covenant to love and honor and cherish time and time again over the course of many, many years, it was I who broke the covenant by acknowledging through divorce what had already spiritually taken place.

Is it possible that, because I have a ring on their finger, my Savior is somehow powerless to save me? I will reply with all confidence that the Lord Himself, in His grace and justice and mercy released me in perfect, loving consistency with His nature – as so beautifully revealed in Scripture.

Now I wonder whether, if I had been taught God's *whole truth* and been urged to trust His Spirit rather than the dogma of a legalistic church, I would have been freed many years earlier. But it is what it is, and God will use my ignorance to serve His purposes going forward. I am eternally grateful that He "causes all things to work together for good." [1]

As well, having come out of that dark experience, I can now clearly see the abuser, the terrorizer, the unrepentant, the reprobate referenced and warned against in Scripture. God does not defend such a one; He condemns him while extending a hand of consolation and protection to suffering victims. Yes, Scripture

---

[1] Romans 8:28

teaches release. It affirms the compassionate necessity of divorce.

It Has Always Been About One Thing: Relationship

Then the Lord God called to the man, and said to him, "Where are you?" Genesis 3:9

We must realize that the love story didn't begin in the Garden. It began long before - before starlight, sea or songbird, before wind or waves, in the heart of the timeless Creator-God.

His design was picture-perfect, and His intent was, well, personal. The idyllic setting was just and only that – a setting. Beyond the beauty and infinite mysteries of creation, God desired something deeper, broader and lasting.

Relationship. The pleasure and delight of an interpersonal, heart to heart connection. He wanted to know and be known, to converse and explore with the free-will creatures He had created – a mutual revelation of souls. He longed to overwhelm us with the gift of His creation and to see us thrive in the love He would daily bestow. He wanted us to know His heart and enjoy all His greatest gifts. Fellowship. Friendship. Intimacy.

He still longs for the same.

Yet, a clever deceiver's tale and a doubting heart are sadly sufficient to break the most loving bond. Though the pair could not hide themselves, guilt, fear, and shame formed a wall that separated them from the One who loved them – the one they had betrayed. What God intended for eternity was broken and overshadowed by a deathly pall.

How can we begin to comprehend the longing, woeful grief in the Father's voice?

"My friends, My children, where are you?"

17

Rather than fall prostrate before their Friend and Lord, they ran away. Their hearts hardened, while His simply broke. But He did not give up. He *never* gives up.

But we know that poor choices exact a price. Even then, it was for love that God called upon a sword-bearing guardian to bar the Garden path, to save His fallen children from eternal suffering. And even before Eden's children left in disgrace, God's plan was set in motion. To bring them back. To buy them back. To love them back.

To restore relationship He chose redemption – a sinless ransom paid to emancipate the Father's sin-bound children.

God was willing to pay whatever price was required so that what He longed to have, longed to give, in Eden could be restored, relished and enjoyed.

Relationship.

He wanted it then. He wants it now. He wants you to have it, too. God's loving pursuit of intimacy began with the first moonrise and will not end until the archangel's final trumpet sounds. He wants to know you. He whispers *your* name.

"Where are you?"

What had been enjoyed in the light of perfection now moved under the shadows of selfishness, guilt and suspicion. In a world darkened by sin, it is unwise to trust myself, let alone another. Yet, God still calls us to relationship – with Him and others. And our hearts still long for intimacy.

We dare to wonder: *Is there someone who can see what good there is in me, someone who can accept me as I am and see what I have to offer, even while I am broken?* We pray it is possible,

18

for that which God ordained in the garden remains something for which every heart yearns.

If we are blessed to find what we believe to be love, we accept it, embrace it, and cherish it. So, marriage is meant to be a loving, mutual bond, a genuine reflection of Christ's love for His bride, the church.

Marriage: God's love lived out.

Marriage: God's Gracious Gift

The man gave names to all the cattle, and to the birds of the sky, and to every beast of the field, but for Adam there was not found a helper suitable for him.

So the Lord God caused a deep sleep to fall upon the man, and he slept; then He took one of his ribs and closed up the flesh at that place. The Lord God fashioned into a woman the rib which He had taken from the man, and brought her to the man. The man said, "This is now bone of my bones, and flesh of my flesh; She shall be called Woman, because she was taken out of Man." For this reason a man shall leave his father and his mother, and be joined to his wife; and they shall become one flesh. And the man and his wife were both naked and were not ashamed.
Genesis 2:20-25

The man was surrounded by beauty, his every need was supplied, and surely he must have been awed by the mysteries and interaction he enjoyed with the creatures that shared his world. But something was lacking. The animals had been paired, male with female. But God wanted the man to have not just a mate like those in nature. He intended for man to have far more than merely an instinctual relationship, but one that is altogether emotional, physical and spiritual. So, God created one for him who was special – a helper, a companion, a complement, a lover.

God takes from man something he does not need and replaces it with something he cannot resist.

All of creation stands ready to receive her, and she is God's exclamation point. Apparently Adam agrees. The man, who could not help but be amazed by all that the good things that God has created, awakens from his slumber to be presented with the highest and best gift: woman. Adam doesn't simply say, "Gee, thanks, God." Emotion fills the pronouncement: *"This is now bone of my bones and flesh of my flesh...*" She was everything he could have hoped for. She was perfect for him. He loved her as himself.

Following Adam's declaration, Moses comments on the foundation of the marital bond: *For this reason a man shall leave his father and his mother, and be joined to his wife; and they shall become one flesh.* Since neither Adam nor his bride had "parents," this side-note emphasizes the intended design of breaking away from the original family unit to form a new one, both physically and spiritually. Moses then returns to his original commentary, noting that, "*...the man and his wife were both naked and were not ashamed.*" This provides a glorious insight into the absolute sense of safety and vulnerability that permeated the relationship. What an incredible image of a truly divine union.

Of course, God knew how perfect it all was; it was His creation, His design. It was the freedom to choose relationship with their Creator that made the bond precious, and it was the free will that broke the same bond. It comes as no surprise then that God's highest institution has suffered as a result of the hard-heartedness and rebellion common to man.

God's Wondrous Design

Wives, be subject to your own husbands, as to the Lord. For the husband is the head of the wife, as Christ also is the head of the church, He Himself being the Savior of the body. But as the church is subject to Christ, so also the wives ought to be to their husbands in everything. Husbands, love your wives, just as Christ also loved the church and gave Himself up for her, so that He might sanctify her, having cleansed her by the washing of water with the word, that He might present to Himself the church in all her glory, having no spot or wrinkle or any such thing; but that she would be holy and blameless. So husbands ought also to love their own wives as their own bodies. He who loves his own wife loves himself; for no one ever hated his own flesh, but nourishes and cherishes it, just as Christ also does the church, because we are members of His body. Ephesians 5:22-30

Here in Ephesians, we see a perfect complement of balance in God's marriage design. The Apostle Paul begins by reminding women to be subject to their husbands, as to the Lord. He then notes that the husband is the head of the wife as Christ is head of the church – the Savior of the body.

If Jesus is the Savior of the body (and He is), so too ought husbands to serve as a type of savior, a protective covering for his wife and family. The church is subject to Christ, and Christ is eternally trustworthy. So a wife should be able to trust the heart of her husband in all things. A husband is to love his wife as Christ loved the church – willing to sacrifice himself in love.

A husband's loving commitment will form the essence of a godly marriage, resulting in all those within his scope being sanctified by his example, strengthened and encouraged. A husband should love his wife as he loves his own body, nourishing and cherishing her. So then, in response to a man who exhibits this loving example, a wife, in return must show her husband the respect he deserves.

Pastor Walter Callison beautifully describes a godly marriage as "…a supreme state of equality."[2] What we see in the balance is a picture of mutual devotion that is realistic and achievable. The kind of relationship described here is one of love and respect.

A godly man wants to see his wife and his progeny content, fulfilled, healthy, safe, secure, confident, balanced and full of faith. A man who lives and leads in faith should have little

---

[2] Walter Callison, Divorce: A Gift of God's Love (Leawood KS: Leathers Publishing), 2002, p. 45

difficulty procuring the good will, trust and respect of others as a result of his godly example. In turn, those under him point to his leadership and godly counsel with honor.

The husband is typically the protector and provider. Within God's design, he is the primary decision-maker, although a godly man willingly receives the counter-balance of input from his wife. The woman's strengths lie in her nurturing tendencies that complement her husband's leadership qualities and her godly wisdom, which gives her husband strength and is a blessing to the entire family.

Some will be offended by the assumption that women excel in "subservient" roles. Women are absolutely capable of taking charge, working in leadership and supervisory capacities, and excelling in similar professions as men. Nevertheless, it seems consistent that, in marriage, the man is to bear the responsibility as the head of the home while remaining accountable to Christ, and the woman is urged to willingly submit to his leadership out of respect, not obligation, for the sake of balance, as she would defer to Christ.

My husband tells people, "My wife submits to my lead, and I submit to her need." This is a perfect way of describing a godly marriage. I know my husband's intentions for me are always good, so it is easy to trust and affirm his leadership, and his ability to lead and protect frees me to act in other complementary roles. He, on the other hand, works to make sure that my needs are met, that I am content and fulfilled, and the healthy cycle of mutual honor is self-fulfilling and God-honoring. I can assure you that my relationship with my former husband was nothing close to what I am privileged to enjoy with my husband Doug now. I wouldn't trade it (or him) for anything.

Now, it must be admitted that either one of us could go off the deep end, become immersed in habitual sin or walk away from

26

our marital bond. But, we have each found exactly what we were looking for in each other and in marriage, and we are *both* willing to do our part to keep our relationship with God and each other on solid ground.

So it is that a man cherishes and nourishes his wife as he would his own body. This was understood from the very beginning, as when Adam proclaimed his adoration of Eve, saying, *"This is now bone of my bones and flesh of my flesh..."* Genesis 2:23 And it follows that when a husband does cherish his bride, a Spirit-filled woman is inclined to respect and submit to her husband, knowing he would do nothing to place her in harm's way, for he loves her as Christ loves the church. She is part of him, and he seeks her good. The complement is wondrously balanced and beautiful.

The challenges of life, with husbands and wives bringing different strengths, weaknesses, lifestyles, baggage and idiosyncrasies, can make marriage complicated and stressful - there is no doubt about it.

Marriage conferences often endeavor to bring couples together to help one gender to better appreciate the needs of the other, and vice versa. Just the stresses of daily life can make it difficult to keep our marital relationship as a priority. We can forget to really see, appreciate and love on one another. A lot can be accomplished when we refocus on communication, emotional connection, compromise, responsibilities, time management, finances, employment, goal-setting, child-rearing, and every other aspect of family life. Times together in prayer and transparency help to heal wounds, open lines of communication and unify couples in the desire to follow our Leader. As long as both arrive at a place where they appreciate and care for the other, there will be no need of nagging or feeling neglected or fearful.

And, since we're talking about people here, it is good to remember that there is no such thing as perfection. When both

27

partners are committed to the Lord and to one another, with realistic expectations and goals, genuine love and affection, and effective communication, marriage can be a blessing that reaches far beyond the four walls of the household. That is what marriage should look like. It should not be a place where fear, confusion or domination resides.

Christian Marriage or Godly Marriage?

"As they have chosen their own ways, and their soul delights in their abominations, so I will choose their punishments and will bring on them what they dread. Because I called, but no one answered; I spoke, but they did not listen. And they did evil in My sight and chose that in which I did not delight." Isaiah 66:3b-4

Isaiah reminds us that the abominations that many attempt to justify do not go unnoticed. Each day we choose whether we will follow God and seek His heart, play the game of religiosity, fall under the wicked spell of legalism, or simply rebel. In virtually every scenario known to man, we know that choices have consequences – even in marriage. We have not been called to live in a "Christian" marriage, which is nothing but a brand, but rather a godly marriage, which is a true descriptor.

God designed marriage to serve as the ultimate, earthly image of His glory, His love relationship. When people see Christian marriages, they should see Christ. Not perfection, but godliness, genuine affection, mutual protection and a unity of purpose.

Our Father God rises in defense of the righteous and holds all authority to release those in any form of bondage. How then can we turn aside and condone sin by our silence when it is His name that is being defamed and defiled within His divine institution? We have been called upon to fulfill a higher, godly purpose. Yet often we are expected to look the other way when the relationship is sabotaged from within and falls far short of the biblical model we have been given, while our God tells us to go to Him for wisdom and sanctuary. He is not blind to the wickedness in our midst.

"Call upon Me in the day of trouble; I shall rescue you, and you will honor Me." But to the wicked God says, "What right have you to tell of My statutes and to take My covenant in your mouth?" Psalm 50:15-16

God sees both the lovers of good and the hypocritical and defends one from the other. In saying so, am I encouraging easy divorce? Absolutely not. I am encouraging repentance, then reconciliation and restoration - in that order. But without repentance, reconciliation and restoration must wait and may be impossible – a result of individual choice. The issue may not be whether we are living in a so-called "Christian" marriage, but whether we are living in a godly marriage. The terms should be synonymous, but many times they are not.

The issue is not whether two people are married, but whether both partners choose to dignify the marital relationship.

Divorce is not the ideal; nevertheless, it may be right, a reflection of truth.

Vows That Are Beautiful - and Breakable

Marriage is to be held in honor among all... Hebrews 13:4

One commentary expounded on this Scripture as follows:

> *"... Let this state be highly esteemed as one of God's own instituting, and as highly calculated to produce the best interests of mankind..."*[3]

Vows do not a marriage make. Marriage is not merely an agreement or a contractual obligation to be tolerated or diminished over time, nor should it ever be accepted as a form of bondage. It is an institution worthy of our highest earthly esteem and, if given a place of honor by those outside of the relationship, then certainly more so by those abiding in it. Yet it is clear that vows and covenants can be made, kept or broken.

We know going into marriage that there are expectations and obligations. A marriage is like an engine that requires both oil and gasoline to run properly. If one party or the other deprives the engine of the elements which he or she has committed to provide, it will eventually, painfully break down. Of course, if genuine repentance is forthcoming, and the missing elements are restored, then the relationship may recover. But there may be loss and serious consequences as a result of habitual failure. Such outcomes are both natural and biblical.

Marriage vows are made solemnly to one another before God and invite His involvement. Although we prefer to identify the marriage contract as a "covenant," it is, in a more accurate sense, a contract. Biblical covenants are solely initiated by God for a specific and singular end, such as the Abrahamic Covenant, the Mosaic Covenant, and the New Covenant in Christ. True

---

[3] Adam Clarke's Commentary on the Bible, originally published in eight volumes, 1810-26) online edition.

covenants are commitments of God to us, and will be fulfilled by Him regardless of human faithlessness, although sanctions and penalties are still warned against and imposed upon those who reject His sovereign lead. David Instone-Brewer, a theologian and author of "Divorce and Remarriage: A Social and Biblical Context,"[4] and other pastoral teachers much wiser than I share this view.

Marriage vows represent *mutual and conditional* contractual obligations. Vows are kept individually, but ultimately the covenant must be honored by all parties to be kept. Marriage comes with specific responsibilities and limitations so that, should one break them, the consequences are understood.

Our vows are understood to be evidenced – fulfilled - by our actions, and we are warned not to take our vows lightly.

Better that you do not vow than that you vow and not fulfill it. Ecclesiastes 5:5

Vows made present both parties with a choice – whether to honor and fulfill them or not. The choice to sanctify the relationship elevates the beauty of it, while removing choice may, at its worst, condemn an innocent spouse to a master-slave relationship and may expect one to keep his or her vows while the other deliberately, carelessly violates them.

For vows to be kept, they must be upheld by all parties to the covenant. Scripture concedes this point.

The Lord said to Moses, "Behold, you are about to lie down with your fathers; and this people will arise and play the harlot with the strange gods of the land, into the midst of which they are

---

[4] David Instone-Brewer, <u>Divorce and Remarriage in the Bible: the social and literary context</u> (Grand Rapids, Michigan: Wm. B. Eerdmans Publishing Co., 2002)

going, and will forsake Me and break My covenant which I have made with them." Deuteronomy 31:16

It was – and is – wholly understood that the vows we make to our partner before God are to love honor and cherish. In Old Testament times, the words were more akin to love, honor and "keep." The obligations should not have to be explained. The marital relationship is intended to be one of mutual respect, honor, love, genuine affection, care and provision. The intent is to do what we know to be necessary and appropriate to nurture and feed the relationship, not to serve ourselves or leave our marriage partner hanging by some tiny emotional or physical thread.

In my case, my husband chose not to esteem the relationship as exhibited through his selfish and abusive behaviors and choices. He began to violate his vows to love, honor and cherish very early in our marriage. On the other end of the spectrum, I also failed to dignify the relationship by accommodating his treatment as though it was normal and consistent with a godly marriage, which it very clearly was not. When I finally fully confronted the evil that had permeated the relationship, the damage had been done. If he had been willing to repent, perhaps the outcome may have been different, but to this day he has made no effort to change his ways and would likely still assert under the traditional church script that I was wrong to divorce him.

The truth is that both of us failed to dignify the marriage. It wasn't aligned with God's intent for marriage at all; it was a big, long, destructive lie.

The vows we offer freely and the very image of the marriage union itself reflect God's desire for genuine relationship and intimacy. I Corinthians Chapter 13 – "The Love Chapter," paints a clear picture of what love looks like. Love is patient, kind, is not jealous or envious, does not keep a record of wrongs. It can survive the deepest valleys.

The chapter also gives clear indicators of what love is *not*. Somehow we are inclined to overlook the contrast, essentially refusing to acknowledge that some married people who call themselves believers overtly, habitually, deliberately refuse to demonstrate love in their marriages. It is hypocrisy. Yet the church often prefers to close its ears and eyes to this reality.

If I speak with the tongues of men and of angels, but do not have love, I have become a noisy gong or a clanging cymbal. If I have the gift of prophecy, and know all mysteries and all knowledge; and if I have all faith, so as to remove mountains, but do not have love, I am nothing. And if I give all my possessions to feed the poor, and if I surrender my body to be burned, but do not have love, it profits me nothing. I Corinthians 13:1-3

Before the Apostle Paul describes the essence of godly love, he first reminds us that the most impressive gifts of knowledge and insight, works of generosity, faith or miracles - even to the point of martyrdom - are of no value if love is absent. Such acts constitute little more than noise - good things that of themselves yield no profit.

Love is not evidenced by words alone. It is not silent, nor is it merely present. Love is engaged, interested, and active. It tends to the needs of its object. It seeks what is best. Yes, love is patient, kind, does not brag, is not arrogant, does not act unbecomingly, is not selfish, is not easily provoked, and does not keep an account of offenses.

Conversely, the individual who is impatient, unkind, boastful, arrogant, behaves in an inappropriate manner, is selfish, easily provoked to anger, or keeps an account of offenses is not exhibiting characteristics consistent with godly love. Very clearly then, marriage partners who neglect, abuse, attack, destroy, manipulate, use, humiliate, physically harm or diminish the sanctity of the relationship have chosen to violate their vows and break the marriage covenant.

A one-sided love does not constitute relationship, and marriage is intended to be the very essence of relationship; therefore, if one fails to love, there is no genuine relationship.

*"This is My commandment, that you love **one another,** just as I have loved you."* John 15:12 (emphasis added)

Love is also a choice. Even the Lord does not force anyone to love Him. He draws us, but we must respond. And even in the face of perfect love, some will refuse that which is offered. This is true in our relationship with God, and it is also true in marriage.

It is believed that as married partners, our responsibility is to love as God does – with an unfailing love that never gives up in spite of the actions of our spouses. And I agree – to an extent.

Each of us must love to the extent to which we are called to love and give and serve. Yet, there also may come a time, just as with the Lord's love for us, when He releases the willful and rebellious to live with the consequences of his or her ungodly lifestyle. Otherwise we only soften the landing for those who would otherwise fall, giving benign approval to their cruel or harmful choices.

Looking at the image of relationship that marriage is to exemplify – that of Christ and His bride, the church – there is mutual appreciation and devotion. Our Savior loved and sacrificed Himself for us, His bride, and we receive His love and fall at His feet in gratitude. Therefore, a husband who abuses his wife and a wife who holds her husband in constant contempt may be living in what may be called a "Christian" marriage, but it is not a godly marriage.

The church has come to stand on the Christian "law" of love and marriage that requires a victimized spouse to remain in a cruel or toxic marriage. But as surely as God ordained marriage, for those men and women in marriages without love, without relationship, He also provided divorce.

God's Purpose Frustrated

"The wise men are put to shame, they are dismayed and caught; behold, they have rejected the word of the Lord, and what kind of wisdom do they have?

"Therefore I will give their wives to others, their fields to new owners; because from the least even to the greatest everyone is greedy for gain; from the prophet even to the priest everyone practices deceit..." Jeremiah 8:9-10

The statement in Jeremiah 8 is stunning. The "wise" men mentioned - scribes - were to be men of extraordinary reputation, responsible for transcribing God's law word for word, every day faced with the holy task to which they were called and feeding on the Word in the course of their work. Yet these very men were found habitually disobedient.

One commentator states succinctly:

> *They have rejected the word of the Lord. It became...a mere code of ceremonial observance.*[5]

They knew the law of the Lord, but lived as though it was merely a formality, a belief that merely knowing the truth was

---

[5] Barnes, Albert, Barnes' Notes (Baker Books, Grand Rapids, MI, reprinted from the 1847 edition), online edition

sufficient rather than recognizing that their motives and daily lives reflected the condition of their heart toward the God they claimed to know and serve.

Here God judged as faithless those who lived at the top rung of the spiritual ladder, if you will. The Lord goes so far as to confirm that these men were at risk of losing their wives and their other earthly possessions as a direct consequence of their dereliction. In this case, it is likely that these men could forfeit everything to the armies of hostile nations if they chose not to heed His warning and redirect their hearts heavenward.

The loss of their wives was considered a dire humiliation, as their spouses were viewed as their highest prize and possession, and to lose them to others who would be spiritually less worthy is an affront of the highest order. Yet, in their poor moral state, God states that because of these men's abject failure to honor Him and His truth, He will give their wives to others. God's declaration poses a legitimate threat to pretenders who knew what was expected of them and chose to go their own way.

Jeremiah's admonition reminds us that even those holding a title or a position of trust or authority are not exempt from the temptation of sin, the lure of power, or the cruel mask of control. There are people who rely on position, power or appearances to cover their deceit. But the Lord sees what others may not. He also possesses all authority to impose consequences consistent with the offense.

He may indeed free one spouse from the other – whether as a punishment for the habitual sinner or for the betterment of the spouse. But there is no question that the divine Intercessor maintains authority over the relationship to remove a wife from under the authority of the undeserving. Such intervention is absolutely consistent with God's nature.

The unfortunate loss of relationship cannot be understated, both between God and man and between husband and wife. Just as God mourned our separation from Him, He also grieves the loss of relationship that occurs when it is neglected, yet He always holds the authority to intervene.

...the salvation of the righteous is from the Lord; He is their strength in time of trouble. The Lord helps them and delivers them; He delivers them from the wicked and saves them, because they take refuge in Him. Psalm 37:39-40

Love or Let Go

"If a man marries a woman and then it happens that he no longer likes her because he has found something wrong with her, he may give her divorce papers, put them in her hand, and send her off." Deuteronomy 24:1 (The Message)

It was understood in Old Testament law that a husband is not to deprive his wife of food, shelter or affection. And a wife is to respect her husband and honor him.

If a man finds something significantly objectionable about his wife and no longer wishes to have her or be responsible for her, it is his obligation to release her. A man purposely makes a decision to take a wife, with an understanding that she will be his companion, helpmate and lover. And his responsibility is to meet her material needs and treat her well. His wife is to respect and care for her husband and to be faithful to him. It could be presumed that, if a man is not treating his wife with dignity and respect, it is because he is not satisfied with her. She is obviously not fulfilling the expectations he has of her, or his expectations are unreasonable or impossible.

Either the husband is justified by the wife's failure to fulfill her responsibilities in the relationship, or she is unsatisfied with his treatment and has the right to petition for release. Whether

40

under conviction of the partner or conscience, a writ of divorce may be issued, and they are both free to remarry.

Ultimately, in marriage, each partner has an obligation to love the other or release him or her. Yet, we have somehow arrived at this odd conclusion that, once married, one spouse may habitually neglect or abuse the other and the innocent party is obligated to live in the role of the victim for years – even to the end of their days. We are also expected to believe that our faith will ultimately turn the wayward party from his or her reproachable ways, rather than admonishing the offender and demanding that he or she either make things right between himself or herself and the Lord - or release their spouse.

What we often fail to acknowledge is that some people appreciate the advantage they hold under the you-can't-leave-me doctrine. It empowers these boors to throw their weight around and leave their family member-victims confused, fearful, bound and emotionally and spiritually destitute. The right words, right attitudes, prayers, a submissive spirit, selfless accommodation, pleas for attention, affection and care may not ever produce righteousness or correction in the life of such a hard-hearted individual. For some who breed fear, the spouse and children merely attempt to appease or submit to avoid confrontation. In many cases, the offender may sense no obligation or compulsion to change.

Since a husband generally maintained to decide whether a divorce was granted or not, the Jewish culture recognized a wife's right to petition the religious leaders or the secular courts to pressure their husbands to either repent or provide them with a writ and release them. Apparently, the church has a role to play in defending God's intent for marriage as well as the mistreated spouse. Many churches, it seems, fail to acknowledge this role. They don't want to take sides.

But Jesus did.

41

You men who are stiff-necked and uncircumcised in heart and ears are always resisting the Holy Spirit; you are doing just as your fathers did. Acts 7:51

Although the Spirit of the Lord is speaking, there are some who choose to close their hearts off from the sound of His voice. They need to know they have an obligation to either love or let go.

Love or Be Let Go

Circumcise yourselves to the Lord and remove the foreskins of your heart, men of Judah and inhabitants of Jerusalem, or else My wrath will go forth like fire and burn with none to quench it, because of the evil of your deeds. Jeremiah 4:4

God calls upon us to be circumcised of heart, true followers, rather than living according to a shallow perception of faith that lacks substance. Self-reliance and pride keep us far from Him, and stubbornness reaps a harsh reward in accordance with His call to righteousness and justice.

But if anyone does not provide for his own, and especially for those of his household, he has denied the faith and is worse than an unbeliever. I Timothy 5:8

Paul's admonishment makes it clear that our obligation to fulfill familial responsibilities is a reflection of the legitimacy of our faith. Neglect was condemned strongly as evidence of practical unbelief. The Apostle Paul also states without apology that the choices we make will have consequences.

Do not be deceived, God is not mocked; for whatever a man sows, this he will also reap. For the one who sows to his own flesh will from the flesh reap corruption, but the one who sows to the Spirit will from the Spirit reap eternal life. Galatians 6:7-8

If a rebellious spouse remains stubbornly defiant and ignores the cries of his or her partner and quenches the voice of the Spirit, there comes a time when what has been sown will bring forth a corresponding harvest. It is the natural and biblical law of sowing and reaping. The bitter tree yields bitter fruit.

A believer sowing to his or her own flesh and neglecting his responsibilities to spouse and family reaps corruption. The faithful partner should not protect the defiant one from the legitimate consequences of his or her foolish choices.

Often the abusive, addictive or neglectful spouse takes advantage of the grace of the believing, righteousness-seeking spouse and sees no need for change. We do the abuser, the selfish and neglectful no favors by endlessly protecting them from the consequences of his cruel and foolish lifestyle choices. If such a one will not release his or her partner, then the faithful one must remove himself or herself and the innocent children from such a person's presence. Yes, God has provided a way.

Shall we defend the office of marriage while neglecting the sanctity of it?

The Divorce Controversy: Marriage Bond or Bondage?

It is not the law that has failed; it is the intentions of men's hearts. Just as God gives us so many good things, as flawed and selfish as we can be, some are quick to twist and pervert God's good purposes to suit our own purposes.

Marriage was not a covenant to be entered into or broken with ease, but rather committed to fully, and with sound conviction and right living. The Lord recognized the impact on the lives of men, women and children, and the understanding that the union was an earthly reflection of the unity divined in the Garden and blessed by God for the raising of godly children.

Although it is absolutely certain that Jesus was emphasizing the unique intent of marriage, nowhere does He indicate that divorce is sin, or that it is never acceptable. In fact, it is worth noting that not once does our Lord forbid the issuance of a writ of divorce *for cause* in accordance with Jewish law. This will be examined in depth.

Scripture reveals our God as One who emphasizes love over legalism, protection for the unprotected, the balanced structure of a biblical marriage and family, and discipline for those who reject sound instruction. Spiritually, the Lord alone judges the motives and hearts of men, and the Holy Spirit personally leads and guides us. On the most personal level, He is our law, and He holds all authority to set us free from any form of bondage.

Let those who love the Lord hate evil, for He guards the lives of his faithful ones and delivers them from the hand of the wicked.
Psalm 97:10

What is Divorce?

Divorce is a legal, public declaration that the contractual agreement or covenant made before God has been broken as a result of sin, whether sins of the heart or deliberate, harmful acts that have adulterated it. Therefore, divorce is a heart issue first, then a legal one. Keeping two people in a dead marriage does not change the reality of its status.

Can a crippled marriage be restored? Absolutely. Genuine repentance and restoration is clearly ideal and possible. However, the Lord is not impressed with outward impressions, and sees our motives. And the Holy Spirit, who works in each believer's life, clearly possesses the authority to declare a marriage obligation fulfilled or to justify liberation, as He did in my case and many others.

"So if the Son makes you free, you will be free indeed." John 8:36

The Old Testament law did not belabor the issue. Divorce was not something to be exercised casually. Should the husband determine that the relationship was broken, he bore the solemn responsibility to provide his wife with a writ of divorce and release her, never to reclaim her, whether for her sake or his. The act of granting a writ was intended to compel the one issuing it to conscientiously consider the life-altering course divorce represented. A writ was a certificate affirming that the relationship was deliberately dissolved. It was essentially written as follows:

"On such a day of the week, in such a month, of such a year, either from the creation, or the epocha of contracts, according to the usual way of computation, which we observe in such a place; I such an one, the son of such an one, of such a place; or if I have any other name, or surname, or my parents, or my place, or the place of my parents; by my own will, without any

48

force, I put away, dismiss, and divorce thee. Thee, I say, who art such an one, the daughter of such an one, of such a place; or if thou hast any other name, or surname, or thy parents, or thy place, or the place of thy parents; who wast my wife heretofore, but now I put thee away, dismiss and divorce thee; so that thou art in thine own hand, and hast power over thyself, to go, and marry any other man, whom thou pleasest; and let no man hinder thee in my name, from this day forward and for ever; and lo! thou art free to any man: and let this be unto thee, from me, a bill of divorce, an instrument of dismission, and a letter of forsaking, according to the law of Moses and Israel."

Our legal system is deliberately structured to ensure that parties seeking a divorce have ample time to work through their issues and consider reconciliation. This assumes that couples have not pursued practical counsel and put forth the requisite energy to restore and heal any breaches in the marriage before a filing occurs. There are undoubtedly some who seek divorce for the sake of convenience, as a matter of unrealistic expectations or to pursue other lovers; however, these must surely rectify their consciences in response to any promptings of the Holy Spirit.

Others seek divorce because, in essence, the emotional, physical and/or spiritual disconnect has already taken place within the relationship. Again, these are ultimately heart issues. Each of us must bear our measure of responsibility for the failure of the relationship, whether due to deliberate destruction, moral failings or passivity. It is a matter that may only be fully addressed between each individual and our Lord and Savior under the leading and conviction of the Holy Spirit. While we may attempt to weigh the motives and judge the actions of others, only God can judge our hearts rightly.

"All the ways of a man are clean in his own sight, but the Lord weighs the motives." Proverbs 16:2

What Did Jesus Mean?

When a man hath taken a wife, and married her, and it come to pass that she find no favour in his eyes, because he hath found some uncleanness in her: then let him write her a bill of divorcement, and give it in her hand, and send her out of his house. And when she is departed out of his house, she may go and be another man's wife. Deuteronomy 24:1-2

Pastor Walter Callison, who did the theological research and explains his discoveries in his book, "Divorce: A Gift of God's Love,"[i] provides what could be viewed as a unique and perhaps atypical perspective on divorce. Among other insights into divorce-related Scriptures, Pastor Callison's book makes a compelling case that Jesus' criticism was never directed at those who had been divorced, nor did He condemn legitimate "for cause" divorce under the law.

Pastor Callison sheds glorious light on the controversy and brings clarity to the dialogue by clarifying the terminology from the original writing within the cultural context. Once understood, the meaning of the discourse both in the Old and New Testaments becomes altogether consistent and clear. A little research into the biblical terminology confirms the consistency of his teaching.

To put Jesus' comments in their proper cultural context, note that the Old Testament law had provided divorce for "just cause." The law taught that cause consistent with an *"indecency of a matter,"* (Deuteronomy 24).

The term associated with "indecency" does not exclusively reference adultery. The term is almost certainly vague as to make it apparent that "cause" should be justified by something significant or seriously inappropriate without attempting to list what those possible scenarios might be. It was a matter of personal conscience and discernment, recognizing that the divorce should neither be easily exploited, nor bound to a legalist's list of potential offenses.

Failure to provide a wife with all understood marital obligations including food, shelter, clothing and conjugal rights also constituted sufficient cause for divorce.

Even a slave woman who was given to a man's son as a wife was to be treated well – just as a wife and daughter within the family. In the event that she was deprived of rightful provision, she was to be released without cost.

If he takes another wife to himself, he shall not diminish [the slave wife's] food, her clothing, or her marital rights, and if he does not do these three things for her, she shall go out for nothing, without payment of money. Exodus 21:10-11

In Jesus' day, the teachings of the *School of Shammai* concurred with the conscience-centered, "just cause" view of divorce.

However, the *School of Hillel* taught what was perceived to be a more practical, if liberal perspective. It rationalized "cause" to mean "any cause at all." So a man might, for any reason at any time decide that he was displeased with his wife and release her (put her away). This had become acceptable even among the religious, and a matter of debate within the culture.

The act of "putting away," reflected the School of Hillel's easy divorce concept, teaching that, if a man didn't want to remain with his wife, he could simply put her – with or without a writ of divorce.

"Putting away" with a writ was often equated to legitimate divorce, although there was not any serious or just cause for the release.

Even more offensive, men often would put away a wife without a writ of divorce. In such cases, she was removed from the household and no longer under the protection or provision of her husband, yet still technically married. Such a woman would be compelled to commit adultery should she remarry. (This terrible form of marital jeopardy still occurs within the Jewish community today. A woman in this situation is called "agunah," which means "chained woman.")

There were a variety of reasons that "putting away" was more convenient for a man. The issuance of a writ of divorce required the return of the wife's dowry as well as reasonable financial provision for a period of time for the divorced woman as appropriate under the law. Avoiding the issuance of a writ reaped a financial benefit to the man in question.

Putting away was an act of convenience and selfishness, which presumably enabled a man to take another wife. In the book of Malachi, to be explored later, God calls "putting away" an act of treachery – betrayal.

The confusion in Scripture lies in translation. To clarify the terminology, the Old Testament Hebrew term that specifically referenced the writ of divorcement is *keriythuwth,* while the New Testament Greek term is *apostasion.*

The Old Testament Hebrew word *shalach* that described "putting away" is in the New Testament the Greek word, *apoluo.*

As can be seen, the difference between *apoluo* "putting away," and *apostasion "a legal, writ-bound divorce,"* is considerable, yet biblical interpretations exchanged the terms loosely without regard to the very different intents or outcomes as they particularly affected women. But the terms are not interchangeable, nor are the outcomes equal.

Beginning in Mark, chapter 10, we will begin to see the cultural and heart issues and the stark difference between 'putting away' and biblical divorce.

Some Pharisees came up to Jesus, testing Him, and began to question Him whether it was lawful for a man to divorce [put away] a wife. And He answered and said to them, "What did Moses command you?" They said, "Moses permitted a man to write a certificate of divorce and send her away."

But Jesus said to them, "Because of your hardness of heart he wrote you this commandment. "But from the beginning of creation, God made them male and female. "For this reason a man shall leave his father and mother, and the two shall become one flesh; so they are no longer two, but one flesh. "What therefore God has joined together, let no man separate." Mark 10:2-9

Remember here that the Pharisees are attempting to trick Jesus, to draw Him into their ceaseless controversies and create division. Where would He stand on the issue of "putting away" a wife as opposed to divorcing her with or without cause?

Regardless of whether the actions were deemed acceptable within the culture, the Pharisees at least knew the law, and Jesus goes far beyond it, pulling back the curtain to reveal motives and the hardness of heart. The Pharisees' question is not about divorce at all, but about "putting away" a wife.

So, rather than answering the Pharisees' question, He responds with one of His own:

What did Moses command you?

Their response: *Moses permitted us to give our wives a writ of divorcement and send her away.* (Consider the callousness of the logic, for there does not seem to be any need in their minds to even have just cause.)

Jesus replies, *"Because of your hardness of heart Moses wrote you this commandment; but from the beginning it has not been this way."*

Grasp the emotion of His statement. His comments are not directed at divorce for "just cause," they are directed at those who were abandoning their wives for any ridiculous or selfish purpose they deemed relevant. In fact, Jesus says that divorce was provided in response to, and as a result of, the hardness of men's hearts. It is a scathing rebuke that moves beyond the law and calls attention to the Pharisees' self-serving motives.

Jesus is *not* saying that those who get a divorce have a hard heart. That very common interpretation and teaching is wholly incorrect. Divorce was specifically provided in the law, not for the benefit of men, but to provide recourse, freedom and the opportunity for genuine relationship for the neglected, abused or abandoned spouse. The hard-heartedness is on the part of the one who has so little conscience or commitment to his wife that he seeks to rid himself of her without cause.

Divorce was provided to protect one spouse from his or her hard-hearted spouse, to free one from the other and allow the opportunity to perhaps be loved and cherished by another. If anything, Jesus is saying that divorce was provided to provide recourse and freedom for women whose husbands didn't want them anymore, not as a tool to legitimize an act that was otherwise unconscionable.

Then our Lord continues, quoting from Genesis 2:24, *"'For this reason a man shall leave his father and mother, and the two shall become one flesh; so they are no longer two, but one flesh.'"* Mark 10:7-8

Here the Lord is reminding them of God's original design, which was for a man to leave his own family and to establish a home with his wife, devote himself to that relationship, come together and live in a committed, one-flesh relationship under the fear of the Lord – an honored and esteemed institution. They had taken the marital commitment too lightly, misappropriated and abused it.

Jesus continues, *"What therefore God has joined together, let no man separate."* Mark 10:9

This Scripture has been used to support the notion that the act of divorce "tears asunder," what God has joined together, but that supposition is also incorrect.

"Let not man separate…"

Once joined in wedlock no one, whether from within or without the relationship, should do anything that will harm or cripple or diminish its value. It must be clearly understood that it is not the act of divorce that tears the relationship apart; it is the tearing apart of the relationship that makes divorce necessary. We have been warned against contributing to the destruction of such a vital relationship.

Then Jesus elevates marriage to its proper place of honor, saying marriage is never going away. It has been ordained by God. Its design is unalterable and its purpose un-malleable. It is perfect and beautiful, and aside from our relationship with Him, there is no relationship of higher value in all of society. Jesus, our perfect groom has gone to prepare a place for us, and He will one day come to claim His bride, the church. It is exactly this kind of mutual devotion that earthly marriage is meant to emulate.

Does God Hate Divorce?

"God hates divorce."

The Scripture said to contain this missive has been – and continues to be – tragically misinterpreted and misused to the detriment of many a suffering soul. So let's take a look at this important text from the Book of Malachi and examine precisely what it is that our Father God "hates," remembering the critical difference between biblical divorce and "putting away."

"For I hate divorce," says the Lord, the God of Israel, "and him who covers his garment with wrong," says the Lord of hosts. "So take heed to your spirit, that you do not deal treacherously."
Malachi 2:16

There it is. This Scripture sends shivers down the spine of believers and unbelievers alike. Those of us who have been compelled to consider and pursue divorce cringe, imagining ourselves on the sidelines with Satan's army, thumbing our nose at the Almighty while we await His terrible judgment. Some remain in horrendous, abusive and debilitating marriages rather than risk abandonment by our Father-God. Sadly, we have been misled by the common and terrible misinterpretation of this important Scripture.

The Hebrew word for a writ of divorce [keriythuwth] is not used here; once again we see the word for "putting away" [shalach], whereby a wife was sent away without a writ of divorce. So this important text is being quoted out of context, heaping another measure of guilt on people already in pain.

Once understood in context, the intent and correction associated with the passage is absolutely consistent with the nature and character of our God who is altogether holy, just and compassionate. The New American Standard version, which is somewhat easier to navigate, is provided below.

Translated correctly, the text reads:

"And this is another thing you do: you cover the altar of the Lord with tears, with weeping and with groaning, because He no longer regards the offering or accepts it with favor from your hand. "Yet you say, 'For what reason?' Because the Lord has been a witness between you and the wife of your youth, against whom you have dealt treacherously, though she is your companion and your wife by covenant.

"But not one has done so who has a remnant of the Spirit. And what did that one do while he was seeking a godly offspring? Take heed then, to your spirit, and let no one deal treacherously against the wife of your youth. "For I hate divorce [putting away]," says the Lord, the God of Israel, "and him who covers his garment with wrong," says the Lord of hosts. "So take heed to your spirit, that you do not deal treacherously."

On behalf of the Lord of hosts, Malachi condemns the hypocrisy of these people who claimed to love and serve God. These people cry out for God's blessing and recognize that it has been withheld, but the men, the leaders and priests of their households have failed to deal righteously *with their wives.*

The Talmud taught that God gathers a wife's tears, another way of reminding their husbands of their responsibility to care for them. So, when the prophet says that the altar has been covered with tears, the men who have failed their wives know precisely what is being said.

My paraphrase: *Malachi says, "God is disappointed in you. What you have done has covered the altar with tears – the tears of your wives. You sense that He is not satisfied with your offerings and pretend you don't know why. He knows what you're doing. God sees that you have dealt treacherously with the wife of your youth, and you act like you haven't done anything. You made a commitment to her, and she is your*

57

*responsibility and your companion…Stop dealing
inappropriately with the wife of your youth. God says, "I hate it
when you put away your wives, and I do not approve of the man
who betrays his wife so." Malachi says, "Pay attention to your
conscience. Stop your treacherous acts. What you have been
doing offends Me."*

The issue here was that men were failing to live up to God's
calling to be men of faith, righteousness and honor. The wives
to whom they had committed themselves had been customarily
cast aside, conceivably so that the men had chosen, not only to
take other wives, but wives who worship other gods, as made
apparent by the prophet's words a few verses earlier.

*"Judah has dealt treacherously, and an abomination has been
committed in Israel and in Jerusalem; for Judah has profaned
the sanctuary of the Lord which He loves and has married the
daughter of a foreign god."* Malachi 2:11

The put-away wives had not been released for cause, nor legally
released by the granting of a writ of divorce. The men had made
a mockery of their marital commitments, just as they had been
making a mockery of their holy sacrifices (Malachi 1), yet they
still believed they were entitled to God's affirmation and
blessing.

God is angered that they are ignoring something so obvious and
contradictory to a life of faith. He wants men and women who
claim an allegiance to God to live up to their responsibilities and
obligations and for marriage to be a beautiful example of what
love looks like. It also seems clear that the collective conscience
of these men had been pricked, yet seared. Although they had
endeavored to legitimize their actions, they knew in their hearts
that God was displeased with their choices, and the Lord had
deliberately rejected their offerings and withheld His blessing.

Little has changed since the days of Malachi's admonition. In today's culture, men or women who have treated their spouses with contempt may not think twice about showing up at church, raising their hands in worship, putting their offering in the basket and praying for God's blessing and provision and wonder why it feels as though God is displeased with them. Maybe it's because He is.

I have heard from many individuals whose cruel, controlling spouses are worship leaders, elders, deacons and pastors, law enforcement officers, judges and others in high standing in their communities. But God knows our hearts and motives – and theirs. He is neither blind to treachery nor those affected by it. The prophetic word does *not* say, "God hates you if you are divorced." God hates situations where men send away a wife without cause or release a wife without a writ of divorce and an appropriate measure of provision. The deliberate and habitual failure to accept, support and nurture a marital relationship is incompatible with God's purpose for His divinely established institution. (Of course, the same applies with the genders are reversed.)

And, as noted in Deuteronomy 24, a man who is dissatisfied with his wife has an obligation to release her so that she may perhaps find favor in another man's eyes and enjoy the intimacy and benefits of marriage – as God intended.

Using Malachi's admonition to keep people in toxic marriages may be extremely harmful and is clearly unbiblical.

The Only Divorce in the Bible

Then the Lord said to me in the days of Josiah the king, "Have you seen what faithless Israel did? She went up on every high hill and under every green tree, and she was a harlot there. "I thought, 'After she has done all these things she will return to Me'; but she did not return, and her treacherous sister Judah saw it. "And I saw that for all the adulteries of faithless Israel, I had sent her away and given her a writ of divorce, yet her treacherous sister Judah did not fear; but she went and was a harlot also. "Because of the lightness of her harlotry, she polluted the land and committed adultery with stones and trees..." Jeremiah 3:6-9

It is the only divorce recorded in Scripture.

God divorced Israel. He loved her, sought her, called upon her to turn from her wicked ways, to honor, love and seek the God who had led her from bondage and granted her victory and freedom. Yet, she willfully wandered away. There comes a point where He removes His hand of protection. Her heart is not with Him. He lets her go.

God rejects license and insists upon relationship. Love doesn't allow us or others to continue on a path of self-destruction. Love speaks the truth and begs a response, but, love cannot demand change; it can only hope for it. Then, love must move out of the way so that the pain of sin and its consequence can hopefully yield its desired result: repentance and restoration.

God refers to Israel as a harlot. Does that mean that every Israelite had committed a physical act of adultery or prostitution? I trust not. It is clear that the *hearts* of the people had turned away from Him, neglected their relationship with Him, embraced other gods, and redirected their attentions that should have been reserved for God elsewhere. The people had committed *spiritual* adultery. So, those who insist that adultery is only physical are missing the reality. The love relationship had been broken by Israel and officially severed by our faithful God who released her.

Isn't the penalty for adultery stoning? The Father could have allowed His people to be destroyed *under the law*, but His mercy

60

merely released them, allowing them to experience the natural consequences of their sinful choices.

Similarly, God understands that when a person's heart has been hardened against his or her spouse, the relationship has been harmed. There are times when, in mercy, we cry out to our spouse to return to the relationship, to repent and turn from the sin, to restore the relationship to its rightful place of honor.

As time passes, we must similarly assert that there is a time when it becomes necessary to release a spouse to feel the weight of his or her choices. They may turn from their wicked ways, or they may not. But the rejected partner not only has a need but an obligation to let them go – to show them powerfully that their choices are ungodly and unacceptable. And here, the righteous One divorces the rebellious.

Just as God's people chose other gods, so do hard-hearted men and women abandon their mates and their faith in practical ways. The Scripture teaches clearly that, the man or woman who does not endeavor to meet the needs of his or her household is, in the Apostle Paul's words, *"...worse than an unbeliever."* I Timothy 5:8

We know that God cannot sin, and He divorced Israel. So divorce is not a sin.

In Defense of His Beloved

Jesus said, "Moses provided for divorce as a concession to your hardheartedness, but it is not part of God's original plan..." Matthew 19:8 (The Message)

Commenting on this verse, Matthew Poole's Commentary states the issue quite plainly: *"... Moses saw the wantonness and wickedness of your hearts, that you would turn away your wives without any just and warrantable cause; and to restrain your extravagances of cruelty to your wives, or disorderly turning them off upon any occasion, he made a law that none should put away his wife but upon a legal cognizance of the cause, and giving her a bill of divorce…and you by your traditions have expounded that law beyond Moses's intention, and made a bill of divorce grantable in cases which he never thought of, nor intended in that law…so as he who puts away his wife, doth as it were divide and tear his own flesh piece from piece, which is barbarous, inhuman, and unnatural. And the law of God was not, that a man should forsake his wife whenever he had a mind to it, but that he should rather forsake his father and mother than his wife; that he should cleave to his wife, living and dwelling with her, as a man of knowledge; not hating his own flesh; loving his wife as his own body, loving and cherishing her, [Eph 5:28,29.] Now how can this possibly consist with a man's putting away his wife upon every little and trivial cause of offence or dislike unto her?*

The Pharisees sought to trick Jesus, either hoping to force Him to take sides in a cultural controversy or see if He would accept the practice of putting away their wives for "any cause at all." They are forced to admit that the Mosaic law required that they not put them away, but provide them with a "certificate of divorce" in accordance with legitimate cause *and* to release them.

This is powerful because in God's economy, there is always order. First things first.

Faced with the Pharisees' test, Jesus in urges them to recount the proper order of things, of which they were fully aware: *"Moses commanded us to give her a writ of divorce and send her away."*

So then, the Old Testament law states – and Jesus confirms - that *If* a wife does not find favor in the eyes of her husband, *then* her husband is to give her a writ of divorce (legal evidence of the severance) *and* send her away (physical evidence of the

62

severance). It is a deliberate combination of actions necessary to provide legal closure and release. Also, if the terms for a writ of divorce and separation were synonymous, then the sentence would have been strangely redundant, saying essentially, *"Moses commanded us to divorce our wives and divorce them."*

Jesus knew that the Pharisees with whom He spoke had ulterior motives. They had twisted the law to accommodate their self-serving ends, and their hearts were uncovered before Him. Like many other encounters, Jesus asks them to assess not merely their actions, but their motives, something they had conveniently sacrificed in the process.

Some say that the one-flesh union means that once bound, always bound. But that is to say that the union is only physical, while God clearly created it to be emotional and spiritual, as well. The one-flesh union recognizes that each partner sees the other as intrinsically essential to the relationship rather than dispensable or cruelly subservient.

The tragedy is that the neglectful, adulterers, abusers and addicts treat their spouses as possessions rather than people. Their victims, feeling unsupported and trapped by the dictates of a well-meaning, but misdirected and uninformed church, find themselves terrorized and their value diminished, often with little hope for recovery. The offending spouse, particularly the one who knows Scripture, may rule with an iron fist or a self-serving demeanor, and uses whatever means at his or her disposal to control and diminish. There is a burden of fear and risk associated with revealing what occurs in secret, for it violates the codes of Christian normalcy and honor to which we feel obligated to adhere.

So we pray for wisdom and direction. We submit to our spouse based upon the conviction that our loyalty and faith will yield the redemption and restoration of our families. But, what if that is not to be, at least not in the traditional sense? What if the church's answer is not God's answer? As Scripture reveals, they are not always the same.

In my dealings with abused women through my ministry, one of the most common fears is not whether the abused or neglected woman can make safe arrangements to leave her husband, but rather whether the church will encourage and support them in the midst of their distress. Often, it is the pastor or lay person from the church who makes a painful situation even more so.

It is vitally important to stress here that nowhere does Jesus condemn the granting of a writ of divorce for cause. Divorce was given through Moses and acknowledged by our Lord, for the hardness of men's hearts makes it necessary.

Should marriage provide a haven for sin?

Beyond Appearances

For certain persons have crept in unnoticed, those who were long beforehand marked out for this condemnation, ungodly persons who turn the grace of our God into licentiousness and deny our only Master and Lord, Jesus Christ…

…These are the men who are hidden reefs in your love feasts when they feast with you without fear, caring for themselves; clouds without water, carried along by winds; autumn trees without fruit, doubly dead, uprooted; wild waves of the sea, casting up their own shame like foam; wandering stars, for whom the black darkness has been reserved forever. Jude 1:4, 12-13

Each one of us is errant in our ways, and as believers we sense our obligation to accept sinners like ourselves and presume that others are likewise pursuing Christ and serving Him to the best of our ability. However, there are times when deceivers and rebels creep into our midst, enjoying the protection and spiritual covering provided by the body although their motives are wholly impure.

Jude, the half-brother of our Lord, makes it apparent that these "hidden reefs" should be identified for what they are, the unseen, direct cause of untold shipwrecks, and they are worthy of God's judgment.

There is a significant difference between a name and nature. It is ridiculous for us as believers to assert that, *"I am a Christian, and I am married, therefore, I am unaccountable to my marriage partner or to the body of Christ for my behavior. I am untouchable. I am un-divorce-able."*

The issue is not whether we are committed to a marriage, but whether we are committed to a godly marriage firmly established in love that seeks to ensure mutual fulfillment and acceptance within the relationship.

If we adhered to the truth of Christ and elevated those Christian marriages that are Spirit-filled, loving, nurturing, and genuine, then these would serve as the beautiful, godly standard that God intends! These would be the marriages that would inspire us to wait until we are spiritually and emotionally prepared to enter into the divine institution, to seek mates who emulate the character qualities we have seen richly exhibited.

Perhaps we might be ever more vigilant to eschew the world's sensual, superficial standards and pursue relationships characterized by cooperation, self-effacement, humility and authentic Christ-centered unity. We would have something beautiful, something godly to emulate. Nevertheless, the church has a tendency to assert that marriages characterized by overt or habitual sin must be preserved in the name of marriage and as evidence of a godly faith, while making a mockery of both.

Abuse In This Church

"Do not participate in the unfruitful deeds of darkness, but instead even expose them..." Ephesians 5:13

One cannot help but be shocked and outraged at the allegations of sexual abuse that have blackened the eye of the Catholic Church in recent years. Now that sins committed in the darkness are exposed to the light, we shake our heads at the innocence lost, and the harm done to the reputations of those who claim to call on Jesus as Savior and Lord.

Not until the Lord returns to redeem the body of Christ will it be perfected. Nevertheless, we are called to acknowledge that which is hidden from view, the "unfruitful deeds of darkness," and expose them to the truth and the healing power of God's light.

If we would rightly condemn sexual abuse within the church, shall we not also rise up to condemn other abuses within the body of Christ? Or will we align ourselves with those who would shield evildoers from their rightful judgment and keep in harm's way those subject to them simply because the harm occurs within the home?

It is with this understanding and desire to bring healing to those who have been hurt that we must acknowledge that there is abuse and treachery that takes place in the church.

This church.

As much as we might prefer to deny it, it is entirely possible that someone within arm's reach of you is in a treacherous relationship. The abuse, broadly defined to include addiction, adultery, neglect or physical, spiritual, verbal, emotional or sexual abuse occurs in secret, and although many of us would prefer to feign innocence, we must admit that at times the church itself has become a blind, deaf, and silent accomplice.

Pastors, Bible study leaders, lay counselors and Christian friends find themselves uncomfortable when they discover families' marital hardships. While believers – most often women and children – suffer, the church body often avoids asking the tough questions. Conversations continue when the news is all good, and there are times when we can adequately gloss over our deep struggles. But, when we discover that the wounds are deep and the options aren't pretty, it is often appealing to offer to pray and walk away, leaving those who desperately need help without any, particularly because we have eliminated God's biblical form of recourse as an option.

Acknowledging that there are Bible-believing people living in dangerous or critically unhealthy relationships is risky business. It's personal business. Surely, the church does not wish to endorse addiction, abuse or neglect any more than it wants to encourage separation or divorce. Too often, it defers to the traditionally safe, "God hates divorce" mantra, tacks on the traditional stay-together-for-the-sake-of-the-children two minutes of marital counseling, and hopes the family can muddle its way through without much more church involvement or, God forbid, intervention.

For abused or neglected family members, an admission of marital brokenness could be messy and controversial. Quite often the abused set out to pretend they're part of a happy Christian family, although lives are crumbling behind closed doors. Those who suffer show up at church week after week, looking for hope, latching on to any word of encouragement, while holding back the waters that threaten to overcome should they dare allow the dam to break. They smile and shake hands and offer introductions and pretend; wanting to look like all of the other semi-perfect families seated around them. There is no telling how many breaking hearts are beating in the sanctuary, for the game is one many of us have learned to play.

My former marriage had all the markings of a Christian marriage: we participated in pre-marital counseling and a 16-month engagement (that should have ensured ample time for discovery). After marriage, we attended church regularly and led a Bible study for young married couples, of all things. Over the years, we had a fairly active social life and added a mortgage and children. But, not long after we were married, my husband began his cruel assault on my emotions through increasingly harsh words and actions.

What began as a now-evident pattern of deception and controlling tendencies gradually intensified, culminating in the ongoing diminishment of my value, dominance and control, emotional cruelty, humiliation, and attempts to isolate me from friends and family and other means of potential emotional support. The abuse became intolerable when his prescription drug, alcohol and pornography addictions exacerbated his abusive conduct, spending addiction, and uncontrolled outbursts.

When the Holy Spirit Himself finally directed me to leave my home with our children, I was on the verge of a nervous breakdown. My then-husband was involved in the worship ministry, as I was, and I had kept his secrets well, believing that I was honoring God and my marriage vows by maintaining my silence and shielding our children and family from the view of outsiders. As a believer coping with the ups and downs of a highly unstable relationship, I prayed fervently, misconstruing the Scripture that, "Love conquers all," and convinced that, with God's help, my love could bring him back. We had met with a number of counselors, none of whom ever identified the abuse. In the end, I thoroughly believed that my faith would enable him to become the man, husband and father God wanted him to be.

I was wrong.

My former husband never hit me, and there are those who specifically told me that, as long as he wasn't hitting me, it wasn't abuse, and my obligation was to stay with him and remain committed with a prayerful, submissive attitude. It was not normal, it was not biblical; it was abuse. And no degree of prayer or submission would impact my abuser's will while his heart remained hardened – as it remains to this day. In fact, my submission fueled and even validated his actions. The more he abused me, the harder I tried. Our marriage and family had become a tragic mockery of what a Christ-centered marriage should look like.

What I did not see then was that we were perpetuating a cycle of sin passed down through generations. After leaving, with God's release, I ended up divorcing my husband. But divorce doesn't necessarily end the abuse. My former husband still looked for ways to torment me and our children and keep a dominant hand in our lives. But, I became stronger and began to heal

71

emotionally and spiritually with the benefit of wise counsel, the support of my believing women friends and family, and the grace of God.

I never considered bringing it up with my pastor. I had no confidence that doing so would be beneficial. For, at one point during my marriage, after discovering a dating relationship my husband had with another woman, he and I met with a pastor at our home church the day after the discovery and obviously feeling completely broken and betrayed.

After hearing my tearful grievance, the pastor asked my husband if he was repentant, which brought a quick, "yes." The pastor then immediately turned to me and said, "Have you forgiven him?" My mouth must have dropped open as I continued to wipe the tears from my face. He added with a salting of Christian guilt, "Seventy-times seven…" I was speechless, and my conclusion was that the church was ill-prepared to deal with people with problems like mine. Nevertheless, under the church's decree, I stayed, but my husband simply worked harder to hide the dark secrets of his life while the abuse continued.

As the years passed after our escape, and my children and I worked through the pain and grief of our past, it was apparent that the Lord had granted me a healthy measure of spiritual insight to see abuse for what it really is. The Lord inspired me to write, "Why Is He So Mean to Me?" a book for women in verbally and emotionally abusive relationships, and my new husband, Doug, and I started a website to reach out to abuse victims. We have been shocked to discover that many of the women seeking help and direction (those who have dared to share their stories with me) are women of faith. It is not uncommon for their husbands to be men of seemingly good standing in their communities.

These victims are wear-worn, hungry for knowledge, hope and emotional support. They have been emotionally run over. They have been faithful to keep their terrible secrets. They have prayed that their spouses would turn from their hurtful ways and loved them and their children. They are disillusioned with marriage and feel abandoned by a church that doesn't understand what they are living with and the kind of treatment they endure on a regular basis.

At times, some have dared to open up a small window into their world and share their pain with the hope of receiving a measure of compassionate support from their friends or church family. Often they are dismissed with trite, condescending Christian lingo that heaps additional measures of guilt and anguish on their heart-sick souls. I have no doubt these well-meaning brothers and sisters have no idea the depth of pain these people are suffering under, or they would offer them the grace and support they so desperately seek.

What is truly tragic is that we as believers have accepted – and continue to accept – a church doctrine that is at the very least incomplete and at most blatantly incorrect and destructive. In truth, God's word provides consistent admonishment that the church body must be willing to address ongoing sin in our midst.

As part of my research, I read about several videos taken at a very prominent church in my home state that condemned divorce unless it was justified by either adultery or abandonment. The videos, and the transcripts that circulated when the videos were removed, seemed to imply that physical abuse, even occasional beatings, do not constitute cause for divorce, although separation may be acceptable. The transcriptions of the associate pastor's teachings on the subject may still be accessed online (assuming that they are accurate). But I must offer a footnote to this tale, so please allow a measure of grace as you read and consider.

First, let's look at his *original* commentary on abuse:

Someone asked this out of their heart though, "Does the Bible say it is alright to divorce a spouse who is abusing you. I think that's an excellent question of Scripture.

It's not like you can escape the pain. You think you are. There's an immediate release when you divorce and you think I've escaped the pain but anyone in this room who has been divorced you could come up here and give testimony after testimony after testimony after testimony to say that, no, you don't escape the pain.

There's still a pain there. It's a long-term pain. It may come years later when a son or daughter graduates from high school and they have to get back together somehow and make that thing work. It may come years later as you talk with a new spouse and an issue comes up that had come up in a previous marriage. You don't escape the pain.

And I'd always rather choose a short-term pain and find God's solution for a long-term gain than try and find a short-term solution that's going to involve a long-term pain in life. And I take that to mean, and there are some Christians who disagree about this. But I believe that to mean that if someone abandons you that you are free to remarry.

Now the question is, why doesn't it say anything about a Christian leaving a Christian? The Bible doesn't say anything about that because it doesn't speak as if that would ever happen. It can imagine an unbeliever leaving because an unbeliever isn't going to follow… if an unbeliever leaves you and says, "Hey, you have to stay married to me for the rest of your life. I'm going to go live with this other person, but tough. Or I'm just going to go out and do my own thing and whether it's 20 or 30 or 50 years and you can't remarry" — that doesn't seem right, does it? It isn't even Scriptural. The Bible talks about that.

So adultery is one, and abandonment is a second. I wish there were a third in the Scripture. Having been involved as a pastor in situations of abuse there's something in me that wishes there was a Bible verse that says if they abuse you in this and such kind of way then you can leave them.

I want to tell you, the advice that we give, in our counseling ministries, first of all, if you're in these kinds of situations, I strongly recommend that you take advantage of our lay counseling ministries. Go in and talk to someone and let them minister to you.

The advice that we give is not divorce but separation. You should not put up with the abuse. There is nowhere in the Bible that says you should put up with abuse. There is nowhere in the Bible that says it is an attitude of submission to let somebody abuse you. That is not submission.

And so we recommend very strongly, separation. Why do we? It's the only way to healing, because there's an abusive cycle that's been set up. Separation combined with counseling has proven to provide healing in people's lives.

Now whenever I talk about divorce, I talk about it with a great heart for what many of you have been through. Because I realized many of you look back on your lives, some of you were divorced before you were a believer in Christ. Does God hold you accountable for that like He would hold a believer accountable for that? No, of course not. You didn't know. He doesn't hold us accountable for what we don't know.

So what if you were divorced after you were (sic) a believer? And as you look back on it now you'd say "I told myself it was for a right reason but I realize it was more my selfishness than anything else." You have the maturity to admit that. I would remind you that although divorce is a sin, God forgives sin. There's (sic) lots of sins out there. I've got to tell you, without

God's forgiveness in my life, not just before I became a Christian, but after I became a believer, I'd never make it into heaven, would you?

I say that, not to excuse divorce, because God hates divorce. But just to let you know the heart of God about this.[ii]

Well, based on what I have shared to this point, you can imagine that this pastor and I are not always in agreement.

Even after my husband and I separated, then divorced, my former husband did not let up, leaving deep wounds in our children's lives that have taken years to heal – and some may never. If we had stayed, I wonder if I would have had to spend some time in a mental hospital, and my children might have all have ended up on anti-depressants or anti-anxiety medication or illegal drugs just to ease their pain. [I am not implying that such outcomes are unavoidable, but the risk certainly increases.]

God has affirmed and blessed my divorce, my re-marriage and our family a hundred times over. None of us who were spared would have it any other way. And, while the pastor issues a blanket decree that divorce is a sin, you will not find that anywhere in Scripture.

Let's take a look at the pastor's other pronouncements.

This one's on divorce. It pretty much follows the traditional church script.

Somebody asked here — and then I'll go out there for another question — a question about divorce. "If my husband is having an affair and still lives in our home, is it okay for me to file for a divorce if he won't?" The Bible says, "yes." Jesus said, when He talked about divorce, that, obviously, divorce hurts the heart of God, deeply hurts the heart of God, God says He hates divorce because He knows how much it hurts His children. You

76

hate anything that hurts your children don't you? God hates divorce because He knows how much it hurts His children.

When Jesus talked about divorce He said, don't do it, He said, except for the cause of unfaithfulness. It's almost as if He's saying, well if the person is not married to you anymore, if they're deciding to live with somebody else, to have sex with somebody else, they've already made their decision. You can't force another person to unmake that decision.

And this idea that somehow the husband has to file for divorce if he's having an affair, there's nothing in the Bible about that. If your husband is having an affair, and I would say, refuses to talk about it, to go to counseling, to try to work through the marriage, then the Bible says that you have the Biblical right to file for a divorce.

Now a Biblical right doesn't always need to be taken. I don't know the situation, and I don't know the circumstance, and I hope that you've been to our lay counseling if this is about your life or that you've encouraged your friend to go to lay counseling if this is about their life, so they can sit down and talk about the specific situation.

Because the truth of the matter is, I know many, many people who have survived an affair. It was a great hurt to their marriage, but they realized through that what their marriage had become; just two people living in the same house. They also realized what their faith in Christ had become; empty, because obviously there's a selfishness there, that's apart from faith in Christ. And so they came back together and recommitted to Christ and recommitted to one another. That can happen. It's not easy. It's not easy, but that can happen.

And obviously, God is a God of grace. That would be, I believe, His preference for that to happen but you can't force another person to change their mind. And if they've decided "I'm going to be with this other person and yet I'm still going to be married to you," – First of all, I wouldn't be in the same house. I'd ask for a separation immediately in that situation because they are in essence using you in that situation. And you need to say immediately, "I'm standing up because I want this marriage to work." But then I would also say to you that you need to work towards what is going to happen next.

Now if you asked a lot of other questions the answer wouldn't be so easy. If you said, for instance, if my husband never paid me any attention, the Bible talks about sacrificial love, he's a Christian, but he's – and you're not saying this with bitterness, you're just saying this honestly – he hasn't done a sacrificial thing for me in the past 20 years that I can think of. He wants me to serve him, he wants me to respect him, but he never sacrifices for me. Are you able to get divorced in that case? No. Not Biblically. You can; I mean, you can make that choice. But there's no Biblical reason for divorce in that case.

I've learned to be real careful with my words when I talk about this. Even when somebody writes, "My husband's having an affair." I don't know what that means. That's why I said you have to get together... Sometimes somebody... When you're giving somebody advice, and they say, "My husband's having an affair," ask "What does that mean?" Because sometimes they mean, "Well, he goes out to lunch with his secretary." I've seen that happen. "He's having an affair of the heart." That's what they mean. But they couch it in terms so that they'll get the answer they want from you as a spiritual leader. And then they'll say, "Well, my small group leader said it was an okay thing." They didn't tell you really what was going on. They couched it in different terms.

And so if you're talking about someone being involved physically with someone else, Jesus said, "They've sinned in such a way that they don't want to be married to you anymore." And you can't force another person to change their mind.

78

That's one of the Biblical reasons for divorce. The other is in I Cor. 7 where Paul says if they abandon you, if they leave – not emotionally abandon you – but if they pick up and leave and they're not living in the house anymore and they won't file for divorce and they say, "I don't want to be married to you but I'm not doing anything about a divorce," Jesus says, "They've abandoned you." You can't force another person to change their mind.

This is a painful subject. It really is a painful subject. I don't know all the ins and outs of that question which is why I encourage you to get with somebody individually, because I've found that when it comes to this issue of marriage and divorce the only way to really get to good advice is to get with the person who's going through it, look them in the eye and give them some answers. I can give you the Biblical reasons but I can't give you Biblical wisdom without sitting down and talking about it. So find somebody or help your friend to find somebody to sit down and talk with.[iii]

Of course, as a verbal/emotional abuse victim, I am troubled by the following comment:

"When I say physical abuse, I mean literally somebody is beating you regularly. I don't mean they grab you once. I mean they've made a habit of beating you regularly. You need to separate in that situation, because that's the only thing that's going to solve that."

Perhaps he didn't mean the words do come out the way they did, but they certainly give the impression that, based upon his understanding, a smack once in a while doesn't necessarily constitute abuse. Would our Lord agree? In the pastor's defense, I suppose, he advocates for separation and counseling as the only path toward healing, but not divorce unless one of the two qualifiers are met. He contends that those who have sought

79

or obtained a divorce will ultimately regret the decision and acknowledge that the real pain will never go away. Perhaps that is true for some, but it is irresponsible to presume this will be the likely outcome – or the only one. He also falsely claims that it was Israel who sought a divorce from God, while it is clear that it was God who divorced Israel as a result of her ongoing, willful choice to break the covenant He had with her.

And, there is nothing in Scripture to suggest separation as a solution to abuse or neglect in marriage. I cannot find that in Scripture, nor does the pastor provide any. In fact, prior to going to print, I e-mailed the church to inquire as to whether the leadership and the pastor in question still embraced the teachings on divorce as taught in the class. I was pleasantly surprised to receive a response from the pastor himself a few days after I sent my message, which I found very gracious. And the day after I received his response, I also received more than one phone call from a church representative who wanted to confirm that I had, in fact, received his e-mail, which demonstrated a desire to ensure that his effort to clarify his position was successfully relayed.

The pastor shared his concern that his views had been misconstrued, and he followed up with his conviction that abusive relationships may well merit separation. He also confirmed his belief that some situations would "never be safe to go back into;" however, he didn't use the word "divorce" once in his message.

I'll admit that I was appreciative of his apparent open-mindedness about the subject and thought it appropriate to respond and probe a little further. In my response I shared my appreciation for his willingness to respond personally and then added the following (in part):

I would like to offer my observations. You reference the wisdom of separation in the case of abuse, and also note that "there are some situations that will never be safe to go back into."
I agree with both statements, but must ask in response two pertinent questions:

1) What is the Scriptural basis for separation? From my study, there is none.

2) If there are situations that will never be safe to go into, who decides when that is the case?

I never received a response to my questions or comments. I realize this issue has already garnered this man a good deal of unfavorable attention, and perhaps he prefers to avoid engaging in anything that might land him in the hot seat again, regardless of whether the discussion has merit or not. I get that. Perhaps he wondered who the heck I think I am as a divorcee with no theological training whatsoever to be questioning him on such matters. I have no way of knowing for certain.

I also understand the church's desire to avoid lending support or credence to anything that might support easy or casual divorce. Yet the church's role should be to point believers - and unbelievers - to God and His truth, not to attempt to control people through guilt. As God's people, we absolutely have a responsibility to weigh our motives and ask God for wisdom and pray for discernment and direction. Then any decision we make is between us and God.

God has placed in my path others who attest to circumstances similar to my own - Christian men and women who strived to be faithful and survive in the midst of abuse, under the judgment of the church who were ultimately affirmed and released not by their friends, their family members or their pastor, but by the Lord Himself.

Surely, unless you have lived through verbal, emotional, spiritual or physical abuse, adultery, neglect or addiction, it is difficult for believing brothers and sister to even contemplate that to which I am referring. The following is a true account sent to me by one of the women who has contacted me for support and encouragement. This is just a small taste of the kind of behavior that constitutes the kind of treachery that is very likely occurring under your very nose, in your church family.

And, he has never hit her.

Gwen's Story

(This story is shared with the permission of the writer. Names and circumstances have been revised to protect the identity of this woman and her family.)

It all started back in May of 1990. This is the year I met my husband. I was 17. I was nearing high school graduation and worked in a local restaurant. This is where I met Frank. I remember a mutual friend of ours telling me Frank was interested in seeing me and wanted my phone number. I decided it wouldn't hurt to talk to him. (What did I know? I was 17.)

And, so it began. He phoned me every evening, and we talked. I am timid by nature. I can and will hold a good, lengthy conversation, but I am self-conscious when walking in a crowded room. The first evening we did anything together he asked me to ride around town, or go cruising with him. I did choose to do this after I got off of work. When it was time for me to go home, which was in a nearby town about 15 minutes away, he decided to follow me home. He said this was to make sure I got home safely. (Now I know better, but back then I was 17 and thought that was "sweet.") Every day from that day on he has been a part of my life. When I worked, many evenings he would come in the restaurant and order something. After he ate, he would sit in the restaurant and just watch me. I did not see anything wrong with that back then. Again, I thought it was "sweet" that he loved me so much he wanted to be near me all the time. Only a few months later, he asked me to marry him. As a young girl, my dream was always to marry, to be a wife and have children. That is who I am. What I saw in this guy was a way to fulfill my dream.

I cannot tell you that I loved him, although I must have, because I agreed to marry him. I cannot say that looking back now I ever felt loved by him. I thought he loved or cared about me because he was constantly around or near me. For all I knew that constituted love.

I do remember while he sat and waited for me to get ready to go out, we had a disagreement because one of my schoolbooks was sitting out. He had gone through my book and found a note I had written a friend. He questioned me about it. I was shocked he had gone through my book, although again at that time I was not alarmed by it and thought it was a further demonstration that he cared so much for me to look at my books and see what I interested in. I decided that, because he wanted to spend so much time with me, it must be love.

Before we married, I began having feelings that maybe I shouldn't marry him. But, as I said, marriage was my dream. And I was even more timid back then. All our friends and family had been told, the plans had been made, and I felt it was too late to back out. So I went ahead and married him, doubts and all. I was 19 years old.

The first week after we married I remember feeling that I had made a mistake. In fact, I cried on our wedding night. I decided that although my dream was not exactly as I planned, I would make the most of it.

I was raised a Christian and I was in church every Sunday. My parents were strict, and I grew up being told and learning that divorce was a bad thing, and you didn't do it unless you faced extremely terrible circumstances, like physical abuse. I recall in marriage counseling that the preacher required before marrying us, that we both understood that "divorce is not an option." This was drilled into my head, my heart, and soul. "Divorce is not an option."

Immediately after we married, he began mistreating me. There were many arguments and many tears shed. I was crying all the time. I can recall many times that I would be just devastated by

84

him, and I would look over at him only to see him laughing at a television show or tapping his feet to music. I wondered how he could be so happy while I, his wife whom he said he loved, was devastated.

I've endured his cruelty for more than 18 years. I got used to it. About a year after we married, I decided I didn't want to live that way anymore. And we did not yet have any children. I decided to pack my things and go home to my mom and dad.

But, my parents were not happy to have me back home. My mom told me that I had made my decision, that I had chosen to marry him, that I had made my bed, and now I needed to lie in it. She was my mom and surely she knew what was best and I believed that I needed to listen to her. So that is exactly what I did.

I learned to swallow all of the pain and hurt and do my best to make this work. About 4 years into the marriage, Frank decided he would allow me to become pregnant. As soon as I became pregnant, I became sick - very sick. There were times I was ill 24 hours a day. Rather than Frank helping me, he was annoyed at me. I could not understand this. Here I was sick, and carrying his child, and he was annoyed that I could not do for him. I still managed to work when I could, although I was sick.

About 2 months before the baby came, I quit work. We had decided that I would stay home and raise our kids. From the day our child was born, it was apparent that the baby was my responsibility - only. The baby had trouble sleeping, and I was criticized for doing something wrong.

I was made to feel like I was weak if I needed his help. Wasn't he doing enough by earning the money? I had to respect that. He had to go to work so how could he be expected to get up with the baby at night? I was lucky, I got to stay home (he reminded me regularly). There were days I went over 24 hours with no

85

sleep, and no relief or help from him. There was no point in asking; to do so would just give him cause to criticize me.

I decided this is just how men were, that babies were moms' sole responsibility, and I just needed to get over it. I supposed that strong women were able to completely take care of the household responsibilities and they should not have to ask their husbands for help. When I did ask for help, I felt that I was weak, and I was put down for asking.

I do remember at one point packing up my vehicle and preparing to leave him. Frank pretended to phone the police, which terrified my son, and proceeded to tell them that his wife was hysterical and was trying to leave with his son. It didn't matter that he was frightening our child; he was going to get his way. He also disconnected something in the car's engine so I could not drive the car. This was one incident. In the end, I took responsibility for it. I decided that I shouldn't have done that, had lost my temper and things got too far out of hand. It must have been my fault.

I realize now that I made a mistake. The feelings and fears I was experiencing were completely justified. I wish I had left at that point. When our son was about 9 months old, I took him to the doctor for a routine appointment. I started crying while with the doctor, and he asked what the problem was. I explained that I was depressed and upset a lot and cried constantly. So at that time he put me on an anti-depressant. The pill became my wonder drug. The drugs dulled my feelings and senses to the point that I just ignored the terrible stuff Frank did to me. I learned not to speak and just to tolerate as much as I could. I just did things his way, the drugs allowed me to be able to forfeit my thoughts and feelings, so that I could please him. Things went rather smoothly when he had his way all the time, when I did everything for him and to please him. Now I no longer take any medication.

86

Please understand that I believed that what I was doing was right, that I was his wife and that I should submit to him. This was the way things were supposed to be, or so I thought. He allowed me to become pregnant again when our son was about 3 years old. I remember though while pregnant with my second son, I became ill again, only this time I also had another child to care for. One day I had thrown up for over 24 hours straight. I decided I should call the doctor since I could not keep anything down, and it had been over 24 hours. My doctor told me to go to the emergency room. So I had to phone Frank to ask him to come home from work to care for our older son while I went to the hospital.

When he came home, I was in trouble. How dare I bother him while he was at work? Didn't I want to eat? So even though I was so weak I could hardly walk, I got in the car and drove myself to the hospital (while pulling over to throw up on the way). I stayed in the hospital for 4 hours while they re-hydrated me and did some tests and got the vomiting under control. The doctor gave me written orders that I was to stay on bed rest for 3 days to rest and recover. When I got home and Frank read the orders he laughed and said, "Why in the world would a doctor order bed rest for throwing up?" So, I went back to caring for my older son and managing my other responsibilities.

There was never any rest for me, except at night when my oldest son was sleeping. When I gave birth to our babies, I was the one who got up and took care of them. Even on my first night home from the hospital. When my second-born son was a year old, I started working part-time again. There was a shop down the street from where we lived, I knew the woman who owned it, and she asked if I wanted to come there and work part-time. I decided this was a good thing. I took my boys with me from time to time, and I had a babysitter to help me out as well.

I always took every effort to never ask Frank for help unless I was desperate, because there was always a price to pay if I did ask. Asking for any help from him meant I was weak and couldn't handle my responsibilities on my own. I also learned while pregnant with my second son that my dad had a terminal cancer. He had about 2 years to live. This is something else I was expected to deal with on my own. There was never any support from him.

At the same time my dad was ill, my mom became ill, as well. She had a respiratory disease. Frank complained constantly about me needing to go and care for my parents. He complained that one of my other "lazy" family members should do it and not me. But, I wanted to be with them and help them when I could. I tried to care for them when it wouldn't interfere with my other responsibilities. It was very difficult. I would stay home with my boys during the day, and would do all my duties and prepare supper and clean up. After Frank came home, every other day, I would go and visit my mother in the hospital. I would get there in the evening and stay the night with her, and I would come home before Frank had to leave for work in the morning.

My mother was dying, and I wanted to see her and spend time with her before she died. Frank fought me about going to see my mom. He said I should not be out at night. One evening before I went to see her, he told me that if someone raped me while I was out, to not come crying to him, that I deserved it, because I should not be out late at night by myself and that a cell phone wouldn't save me. So, I was not only dealing with my mom dying, I was dealing with all of this from Frank just because I wanted to be with my mom before she died. This is something that to this day, I don't think I can ever forgive him for. My mom died the same year, and I never got to go be with her or take care of her without worrying how upset Frank would be with me. The cancer took my father's life about 6 months later.

To this day, I wonder how I have survived it all. I have endured a deep loneliness and heartache I can't even begin to explain.

About a year after my dad died, I became pregnant with our third child.

Again, it might sound ignorant to you now that I would have another child. At this point I figured I was stuck with him no matter what, and I suppose I still must have had some feelings for him. I gave birth to a daughter. I continued to work part-time in the shop and the rest of the time took care of our children and home. One of Frank's biggest gripes against me, or the thing that I get punished for the most, is time I want or need to be away from home, alone and without the kids sometimes.

My biggest love outside of my children, my only hobby I leave home for is music. I have loved music since I was a child. About 3 times a year I go to see a concert. There is a singer in particular that I like to see. This is Frank's biggest complaint. I rarely get time away. These concerts are the only time I leave my family behind. I recall once I was getting ready for a concert and Frank had to leave the house before me. He told me he wanted to see the clothes I was wearing before he left the house. I was not to wear the jeans that made me look good, I was told.

A couple of years ago, Frank had a big barn on our property torn down. I liked the barn and did not want to see it torn down. He made plans to excavate the barn and even had people called to come and remove the wreckage before I knew a single word about it. Frank was able to convince the insurance company that the barn was wind damaged, so they paid what they thought the barn was worth. He took this money and placed it into a separate account that only he had access to. It was $15,000. He had checks that he hid from me, and he made all of the decisions as to how the money would be spent. My children needed dental care at this time, and I asked for enough money to have that taken care of. I was told no, that money was for the house and would not be used for anything else. I did brave up enough to tell him that I hoped what he had done would be worth the price. I was upset over this, and I was decent to him, I answered

89

questions if he asked and talked to him if needed, but I didn't go out of my way to talk to him for a few days.

He left me a few voice mails which I have saved. They say, "It's me. I am going to leave a message because I can't write, and you know it. Here is the deal. I'm tired of this. Either get over it or get out. If all of your girlie friends tell you to leave, go for it, move out. I will tell you this: you're not using me for the next ten years just because you think you can. If it doesn't change in a few days, I am having my checks given to me in cash, and I will pay the bills. So decide, get over it, or move out because I am not going to live like this. I can't believe that you have stooped to erasing text messages and calls off of your phone. Do you really think I am that stupid? You are erasing messages and hiding stuff so your husband can't see it. And it's sad."

I am glad I have these messages. They prove that he is not the wonderful and caring man that he claims to be. Because I am sure so many people will never believe me because he has a spotless reputation. Over the last year, he had a new roof put on this house that we did not need. We had a metal roof on this house, but it wasn't good enough for him. He wanted a shingled roof. So with no word to me, he spent $3,500 to put a new roof on this house. He had everything planned out before I was ever told about it. (He is a carpenter and had his friends assist with the roof.) He also bought a new 4 wheeler, (for the kids he said but I know better) which was another $3,000. He cheated and lied to have our upstairs redone as well. This was many thousands, and I am not even sure how many. Keep in mind that my kids still need dental care. I need dental care. He does not care. What is important to him is what he wants. How our home looks is more important to him than our health.

I need to add that Frank is very well-received by the community. He holds a place with the elders in our church. He is respected. He will help people in our church for no money. Now he will complain to me about not getting paid, but not to them. He has shoveled snow for the elderly. You can see the contrast in this, and in what I have told you. At church, he helps with a Wednesday night class that both of my boys have been in. Both of my children have been upset at various times over how he treats them worse than the other kids in the class. They told me he favors the other kids over them. He chooses our kids last to help with the snacks and things. They have oftentimes cried or been upset over issues like these.

His moods swing like crazy. One day he will sit in the chair and read a book to our daughter, the next will get onto her left and right and she will ask me if he hates her. She has asked me more than once if he hates her. Another time she asked, "Does Daddy like me, does he love me?" She is 6 years old. My oldest son, sadly, now that he is 14 is becoming somewhat like his dad. I believe he has narcissistic tendencies about him. But he is only 14, so this is hard to see if he is being a selfish teenager or if he is narcissistic too. He treats me with the same disrespect as his dad does. I want counseling for him and I hope this will change. My middle son is not like his brother or father.

Last summer, we were having a disagreement. Frank was harassing me because he had gotten into my e-mail and read about me planning to go to another concert. As I said, he despises these concerts and does not want me to go. He told me that if I thought I was going to follow my "boy toy" all over the United States, then I had another thing coming.

"You can find another place to live, Woman," is what he said. I told him he was not my boss and that I could go if I so chose to go. My kids and I were at a friend's house and my kids were admiring her animals. He kept repeatedly texting me and telling me he wanted me to come home. I told him I didn't want to come home at that time but would in a while. He got mad because I wouldn't come home at that moment and stormed over to my friend's house. He started yelling at me in front of my friend. Talking about how it was wrong for me to go to concerts and

that I shouldn't be on the computer e-mailing and talking about him.

Seeing him blow up at that time opened my eyes. I have never felt the same since then. At that point, I wasn't sure what I was going to do. I thought about leaving and told him that if he ever pulled anything like that again that I would leave without even thinking. I went home for lack of not knowing what to do at that moment. But that day, everything changed. I did a search on emotional abuse on the Internet, and it opened my eyes. I discovered that what had been going on all of my married life was abuse. I was in shock. Slowly but surely I discovered narcissism too, and realized that he is indeed a narcissist as well as an abuser. Ever since that day, I have been learning and educating myself.

But before I knew what exactly was going on, I told him I didn't know if I loved him anymore, that my feelings had changed. He flipped out. He began not sleeping at night. He would kneel down at the side of the bed and would not let me sleep. Sex is a big thing. He bothered me at night until I gave in and slept with him again. He declared he wanted to go to counseling. So he phoned his friend and asked them about a counselor. (He did all of this without my knowledge.) I asked him later why would he even bother his friend about a counselor and why didn't he just look in a phone book? Well, I found out later from a mutual friend, that he had told his friend we needed a counselor because of my "concert obsession." He told them I have sexual fantasies about a particular musician, and I can't get him out of my mind. He also said I spend hours on the computer chatting within his fan club, and that I neglect our children. None of this is true. Our children are here, and I home school them.

So this is the man who is supposed to be changed and supposed to love me and go to counseling and get help. He wanted me to go with him to counseling. He didn't want to go alone. He never will because he thinks it's me that needs the help. During this time he had days of trying to be nice. Then he would yell and rage and tell me I didn't appreciate all he was trying to do, that I was treating him like crap, although I answered every text message and had slept with him against my will.

Also during this time he once prevented me from entering the house. He held the door shut so I couldn't get inside. Also when we were outside he wouldn't let me get past him to come inside the house. There were days he would text me relentlessly. Many days there were at least 50 messages. In order to get him to start acting somewhat normal again, after the fallout last summer, I began to return the "I love yous" and things like that so that I could put my life into order and be able to financially support myself and my children. I did this so he would return to more normal behavior. I convinced him to go to the doctor as well and he was put on an anti-depressant medication that he still takes. My feelings never returned, and they won't no matter what, but yet I am acting right now because I have to.

I am not stupid, and I won't leave my kids out on the streets or lose my babies because I didn't prepare well. Also, I saw him kick a cat, (his mother's cat) so hard that it hobbled off and never came back (he probably collapsed its rib cage and it went off and died alone) and he never even blinked an eye. He threw a stick at our dog the other day. My son asked him why he would do that, and he told him that the dog was not to bark at him, and the dog was lucky that he didn't hit her over the head with the stick and not just throw it at her.

With regard to finances, he puts his work check in the bank, and that is what I am to pay bills with. I get questioned about whether or not certain bills have been paid. He also does plenty of side jobs to where he is paid in cash. I do not see this money. He saves this money as his own, and where he puts it I do not know. As I said before, he doesn't care that we need dental care, but spends on what he thinks the house needs.

93

He lies. I had paid all of the bills, but needed some money to take our daughter to the doctor. When I asked if I could have some more money, he told me he had no money, but yet I knew full well he had more than $500 in his wallet. I am required to pay certain bills with what he puts in the bank, and there are times we have had to go without groceries to pay the bills, but yet he always has a fat wallet for himself and money to go eat out if he so chooses.

I also wanted to explain to you more about how he is in regards to intimacy. He will not approach me for it. He expects me to come to him and ask him. If I choose not to after a week or so, he starts with his moods around the house. He is rude to me, mean to the kids, (hence this was one of the times my daughter asked me if her dad hated her). He makes it hellish to live here if I do not sleep with him. He sends me dirty text messages. He does this to provoke me into sleeping with him. I know when I start getting the messages that it is time again. He has taken pictures of me from behind and he sends them to me. I have clothes on but he will snap pictures of me bending over on his cell phone. My kids have told me that he will have a picture of my behind as his wallpaper for his phone. This bothers me profusely. If I don't sleep with him the messages and ugliness continue until I do. There is no love. Period. It is an act and that is all. I have never felt loved being with him.

Thank you for reading.

Gwen

Painful to read, isn't it? What cannot adequately be conveyed is the reality that this is the briefest summary of years and years of ongoing emotional trauma. People who haven't been there have a difficult time relating, which is why I asked "Gwen" for permission to use her story – to give others a taste of what an abusive relationship looks like. Some will undoubtedly judge her and list things she should have done better, but we all do the

94

best we can to survive and make it work, while holding to a fierce hope that tomorrow will be better – it has to be. But sometimes tomorrow doesn't come.

Surely, our Father sees what others are unwilling to see.

For His eyes are upon the ways of a man, and He sees all his steps. There is no darkness or deep shadow where the workers of iniquity may hide themselves. For He does not need to consider a man further, that he should go before God in judgment. He breaks in pieces mighty men without inquiry, and sets others in their place. Therefore He knows their works, and He overthrows them in the night, and they are crushed. He strikes them like the wicked in a public place, because they turned aside from following Him, and had no regard for any of His ways; so that they caused the cry of the poor to come to Him, and that He might hear the cry of the afflicted... Job 34:21-28

An adulterous heart breaks God's.

Does Remarriage Constitute Adultery?

"It was said, 'Whoever sends his wife away, let him give her a certificate of divorce; but I say to you that everyone who divorces his wife, except for the reason of unchastity, makes her commit adultery; and whoever marries a divorced woman commits adultery." Matthew 5:31-32 (New American Standard Version)

This Scripture has served as the legalists' trump card, the rock-solid, undeniable, absolute authority of our Lord insisting that only in cases of adultery is divorce allowed. Further, His statement would seem to condemn any remarriage on the occasion of any divorce, even in cases of adultery, giving the impression that a divorced person who remarries commits adultery, and the person who marries a divorced person also commits adultery.

The language here seems persuasive, but Jesus' meaning has once again been misconstrued. Even on its face, the response is patently inconsistent with our Lord's nature as revealed throughout Scripture.

It is important to note that His comments are made in the context of the Sermon on the Mount, a discourse where our Lord emphasizes the motives of the heart, not merely adherence to the technicalities of the law. This is important to remember as we move through this section of Scripture. Let's take a closer look.

Blessed are you, the poor in spirit, the merciful, the peacemakers, the pure in heart... Jesus reminds the people that they are not forgotten, and they will be rewarded. *God sees your heart.*

Then He reminds them that they are the salt of the earth and the light of the world. He urges them not to give up, not to become bitter, not to stop doing what is right, to be faithful. *God sees your heart.*

In verse 20, Jesus again emphasizes the contrast between the law and their hearts. He tells the people that the check-the-right-boxes form of righteousness encouraged and taught and lived by the Scribes and Pharisees is not genuine righteousness at all. It is insincere and shallow, and God sees right through it.

"...unless your righteousness surpasses that of the scribes and Pharisees, you will not enter the kingdom of heaven." Matthew 5:20

Jesus is not discrediting the law, but drawing us to look beyond it, insisting that our lives be grounded in genuine relationship and not just regulations. So, to make His point, He begins with the Pharisees' teachings and then leads beyond those check-off boxes – to emphasize the condition of our hearts. *You have been told 'you shall not murder,' but if you look on someone with hatred, your heart is wrong... Check your heart.*

You have been told 'do not commit adultery,' but if you look a woman with lust, you have committed adultery in your heart... God knows when sin festers in your heart.

Shortly thereafter we come to the words the legalists love to trumpet:

"You have been told that 'whoever puts away his wife, let him give her a certificate of divorce'; but I say to you that everyone who divorces his wife, except for the reason of adultery, makes her commit adultery; and whoever marries a divorced woman commits adultery."

At a glance, it seems pretty clear.

But, let's look closer at Jesus' first declaration (paraphrase):

You have been told that if you wish to put away your wife, give her a certificate of divorce and send her away.

Jesus did not say, *"You have been told that if you must divorce your wife for cause..."* No, He said essentially, *"You have been told that if you would like to put away your wife, then give her a writ of divorce and send her away."* (paraphrase)

The discourse is not about the issue of biblical, legitimate divorce at all, but the act of putting away a wife. (See the chapter entitled, "What Did Jesus Mean?")

Although some translations use the word "divorce" rather than "putting away," the only reference to divorce occurs where a "writ of divorce," (the legal document required to release a wife) is mentioned. The other references do not use the word for a legal divorce, but rather the correct translation reads *apoluo,* the term that specifically references "putting away."

Young's Literal Translation more accurately reads:

*"And it was said, that whoever may put away his wife, let him give to her a writing of divorce; but I—I say to you, that whoever may **put away** [apoluo] his wife, save for the matter of whoredom, doth make her to commit adultery; and whoever may marry her who hath been put away doth commit adultery."* Matthew 5:31-32 (emphasis added)

So, first we must acknowledge that divorce for cause is not the issue being discussed. Now, let's break this down further. For, in a single sentence, our Lord's comments address three very specific issues related to the act of putting away a wife. We will take them one by one.

Issue #1:

You have been told that whoever would put away his wife, let him give her a writ of divorcement...

Just because you have been told that you can get away with putting away your wife if you just give her a writ of divorce before sending her away doesn't legitimize what you know in your heart to be wrong.

Issue #2:

...But I say whoever would put away his wife, saving for the cause of whoredom...

The term for "whoredom" can also be translated as unchastity, fornication, immorality, adultery or incest.

Most who teach on this section of Scripture conclude that the word "whoredom" here applies to the wife's adulterous offense. While the statement may support this context, it may also support another.

Jesus may also be telling the men that they may send away a wife without providing her with a writ of divorce if he is releasing a woman with whom he is in an adulterous relationship. The inference supports a situation where a man has put away and is not legally divorced from his former wife, which would constitute adultery and/or polygamy, or if he is in a relationship that constitutes an immoral and unsanctioned living arrangement, including incest, or living with a prostitute, another man's wife, or another woman outside of marriage.

The "wife" you may send away without a writ of divorce is the one with whom you are in an unsanctioned, ungodly or immoral relationship.

The repudiation of such a relationship can be seen in I Corinthians 5 that the Apostle Paul condemns a man who "has" his father's wife, referring to the violation as "fornication." The marriage was not viewed or described as a marriage, for the terms are mutually exclusive. It is impossible for a relationship characterized by fornication to be synonymous with marriage. In such a case, the adulterous partner could be "sent away" without a writ of divorce.

Living in an adulterous relationship, a man can and should send away a woman without a writ because the "marriage" is unacceptable in the eyes of God. This is made very clear by going back only a few sentences earlier. When discussing adultery of the heart, Jesus specifically says *"...I say to you that everyone who looks at a woman with lust for her has already committed adultery with her in his heart. If your right eye makes you stumble, tear it out and throw it from you; for it is better for you to lose one of the parts of your body, than for your whole body to be thrown into hell. If your right hand makes you stumble, cut it off and throw it from you; for it is better for you to lose one of the parts of your body, than for your whole body to be thrown into hell."* Matthew 5:28-30

Jesus was not changing the subject. This entire discussion is intended to address adultery of the heart. His call to pluck out an eye if it causes you to stumble directly relates to the one who has accepted the sin of putting away a wife or living in an adulterous relationship that began with the lust of the eyes.

Ignoring this sin is one more brick in the wall of heart-sin that has the power to separate us from God. Tear down the wall, check your heart, get right with God.

But why would Jesus refer to the woman in the relationship as a wife if she is not really a wife? This wording is perfectly understood, and we can see this from Old Testament judgments in Ezra and Malachi, where the Lord condemns ungodly or polygamous marriages to those who would draw us away from God.

...an abomination has been committed in Israel and in Jerusalem; for Judah has profaned the sanctuary of the Lord which He loves and has married the daughter of a foreign god. Malachi 2:11

The treachery documented in Malachi occurred when men put away the wives of their youth to take other wives who maintained an allegiance to other gods, ignoring the act of adultery they were committing. The prophet Ezra also commands in God's name the putting away of wives from ungodly marriages without a writ, for the marriages were adulterous.

Then Ezra the priest stood up and said to them, "You have been unfaithful and have married foreign wives adding to the guilt of Israel. "Now therefore, make confession to the Lord God of your fathers and do His will; and separate yourselves from the peoples of the land and from the foreign wives." Then all the assembly replied with a loud voice, "That's right! As you have said, so it is our duty to do." Ezra 10:10-12

Then we come to Issue #3:

If the woman you put away remarries, she commits adultery, and the man who marries a put away woman also commits adultery.

The woman Jesus is referencing here, the put-away wife, has not been legally divorced, she has been put away. So the common cry that a divorced woman who remarries commits adultery, and the man who marries a divorced woman commits adultery is utterly backward. The issue is not that the woman is divorced but that she is *not* divorced, and Jesus also makes it clear that the man who put her away is liable for her adultery by not at a minimum providing her with a writ, since she by necessity may

104

be compelled to remarry. Should a man accept her as a wife, he too commits adultery, because she is still another man's wife.

In proper context, the intent of Jesus' words are much more readily understood (paraphrase): *"It has been said that whoever may choose to put away his wife, let him give her a writ of divorce. But I say, whoever puts away his wife - except for adulterous situations - causes his wife to commit adultery. And whoever marries her who has been put away also commits adultery."*

This view not only lines up with Scripture, but also with God's heart – a heart that loves marriage, genuine relationship, truth, righteousness, justice, and mercy.

However one prefers to view this Scripture, Jesus' comments here were not in reference to lawful divorce. Jesus never once condemned or contradicted the Mosaic law as it applies to divorce for cause and subsequent remarriage. He did, however, stress that divorce and/or remarriage were never intended to be casual decisions of convenience, but rather serious matters of the heart and conscience.

Jesus made it clear that it is a hardness of heart on the part of one or another or both marriage partners that makes divorce necessary, while affirming that "it was not meant to be this way."

To summarize, **biblical divorce** is exercised in accordance with *just* cause and is to be carried out with the provision of a writ, or a document affirming legal grounds and permanent release.

Unbiblical divorce could be viewed as one exercised without just cause, even with the provision of a writ.

Putting away is the act of sending away a spouse without cause - with or without a writ. Sending away a "spouse" without a writ is appropriate when the relationship is unsanctioned, consistent with fornication, an illicit sexual relationship that may be adulterous, polygamous or incestuous.

Jesus' teachings were entirely consistent when viewed in light of Old Testament history, culture, context and language.

The Adulterous Heart

You have heard that it was said, 'You shall not commit adultery;' but I say to you that everyone who looks at a woman with lust for her has already committed adultery with her in his heart. Matthew 5:27-28

To the one who knows the right thing to do and does not do it, to him it is sin. James 4:17

First, I cannot resist drawing attention to the fact that, from a legalist pretext, since virtually all of us at one time or another might fantasize about another person, we could all be deemed guilty of adultery. So, perhaps it could be said that, should our partners choose to divorce us, they would *always* have just cause "under the law" as taught by our Lord.

I have yet to hear anyone teach from that perspective, nor is this a teaching to which I would ever subscribe. It is important that we acknowledge then that both the sanctity of marriage and the sanctity of divorce are matters of conscience, directly connected to our heart motives and our love relationship with God.

Even with all of our imperfections, relationship is still not only possible, but beautiful when our hearts are right. And it is the condition of our heart that Jesus once again emphasizes. If we are hateful, we have a murderous heart, and lust betrays an adulterous heart, so that we must choose to identify and correct

106

temptations and ill thinking before acting in a manner that causes injury to ourselves or others.

Conversely, some live under the false impression that, as long as our thoughts do not translate into actions, God is happily unaware of our hearts' condition. Jesus insists that it is in the heart that sin is committed, even if the law might be perceived to accommodate it. We know when what we are doing violates the heart of God, even if we can find a loophole in the law that may not directly identify it as sin.

In our present day culture, adultery in its truest sense is defined as having occurred when a man or woman engages in a sexual relationship with someone other than his or her marriage partner. However, in biblical times, adultery was defined as sexual relations between a man and another man's wife. Adultery was an offense committed only against a man. A woman could make no accusation.

Under this strict interpretation, and as we have seen, a man might take a woman who was not already another man's wife, or a prostitute, and claim that he had not committed adultery under the law. Justifying such an action "under the law" does not make it right. Jesus went far beyond the holes in the law to the heart of it.

Jesus made it clear that adultery can take place in the heart while the body has technically abstained. He also made it apparent that the concept of looking for and exploiting loopholes in the law to justify sin was ridiculous. No law or self-serving interpretation of it can circumvent the reality - or consequence - of sin, which is emotional and/or spiritual separation, the abandonment, neglect or abuse of the relationship.

Since the heart betrays our intentions and loyalties, other heart issues may similarly adulterate the relationship. To "adulterate" literally means "to debase or make impure by adding inferior materials or elements." It could be said that a relationship is adulterated when something is added to it that defiles it.

In addition to sexual sins, there are many other "inferior materials or elements" that can adulterate a marriage, including drug or alcohol addiction, spending addiction, gambling addiction, pornography addiction – even an addiction to technology, and then there is neglect or abuse.

These are all "inferior elements" that debase, demoralize and contradict the beauty of the marital design - sin that begins in the heart and manifests itself in a variety of unhealthy and damaging ways. These are the attitudes and issues that undermine and can lead to the "tearing asunder" of a marriage. Again, while this definition does not adhere to the strict jots and tittles under the law, it makes little sense to discount the obvious heart issues that lie at the core of all relationships. Just as when God divorced Israel, it was because the nation's heart had turned cold toward Him. The act of adultery was not literal, but figurative, yet entirely accurate, and God chose to divorce her.

Although the church often condones keeping families together in the midst of addiction, adultery, neglect or abuse, a passive response to an unrepentant heart is inconsistent with God's design. The Lord is gracious and merciful, yet there comes a time when He turns the sinner over – and He expects us to do the same when dealing with a reprobate, a willful sinner.

It is actually reported that there is immorality among you, and immorality of such a kind as does not exist even among the Gentiles, that someone has his father's wife. You have become arrogant and have not mourned instead, so that the one who had done this deed would be removed from your midst.
I Corinthians 5:1-2

As referenced earlier, here the Apostle Paul identifies a sexual sin where a man has taken his father's wife, (presumably a stepmother) following his father's death. Nevertheless, it is clear that immorality that has been ignored or tolerated in the church body is addressed here. The habitual sinner is to be exposed for his sin, called to accountability and repentance and, in the event he refuses to turn, he is to be removed from the body in the hope that he feels the weight of his rebellion, addresses the sin and returns to the body repentant. The early church took such discipline very seriously. The body was to avoid social contact with the outcast believer, with the intent of not only addressing the obvious sin, but also with the intent of encouraging heartfelt restoration.

Turning a blind eye to obvious, habitual sin is clearly inappropriate. No church should defend the immoral and give the defiant credence where he or she should have none. The ignorant condone by their silence and inaction, refusing to acknowledge or protect the innocent from overtly sinful behavior. In fact, the church has a responsibility to act.

*I wrote you in my letter not to associate with immoral people; I did not at all mean with the immoral people of this world, or with the covetous and swindlers, or with idolaters, for then you would have to go out of the world. But actually, I wrote to you not to associate with any **so-called brother** if he is an immoral person, or covetous, or an idolater, or a reviler, or a drunkard, or a swindler—not even to eat with such a one. For what have I to do with judging outsiders? Do you not judge those who are within the church? But those who are outside, God judges. Remove the wicked man from among yourselves.* I Corinthians 5:9-13 (emphasis added)

Cheri's Story

I have been married for nine years. A lot of the revelations that I have had concerning abuse in the marriage have come within the last year or so. However, there were some areas of concern that have been fairly consistent and then eventually escalated towards the end of the marriage. It seemed that with the addition of each child (there are three) that as the responsibilities increased there was a decrease of emotional and physical support from my spouse.

There was a high level of expectation placed on me. In regard to cooking and cleaning I was expected to have things done near perfection, which is impossible to maintain with any longevity There was constant criticism about my endeavors. When I spoke, I didn't say the right things or my tone of voice wasn't appropriate. I wasn't allowed to express my feelings or concerns. It seemed like every conversation eventually reverted back to my husband's needs and desires. I truly felt alone and dismissed. Despite the circumstances, I still endeavored to be the best Christian wife I could be. After all, divorce wasn't an option. I would pray and ask God to intervene in our marriage. I know that nothing is impossible with God, so I was waiting for a miraculous change in our circumstances.

When I was pregnant with our third child, there were three instances of physical abuse directed toward me. It was at that point that I asked myself, 'What kind of legacy do you want to leave for your children?' I realized that by staying in the marriage I was in effect saying yes to the abuse.

One day while on the computer I googled emotional abuse, and I came across the hurt by love website. As I read, I realized that what I had been enduring was not unique and that others had struggled with the same issues that I had. I could then put a label on my experiences and feelings.

I then began to pray for God to show me HIS WAY and HIS WILL for my situation. Through much prayer, I knew that the Lord was leading me out of the marriage. I had peace in my heart, however I still struggled with my flesh to understand God's Word on divorce. I continued to ask God to show me His way. I understood that divorce could be justified in the case of adultery or desertion. Then you get into the interpretation as to whether God is referring to a "literal" or an "emotional" desertion. In regard to the response of my church on these matters, a person in authority told me that I should pray that my husband would physically leave. In other words, her interpretation was that it needed to be a physical desertion although she did acknowledge that it was an abusive marriage.

When I told my pastor that I knew that the Lord was releasing me from an abusive marriage and had given me a clean conscience, I was told that "God hates divorce" and that I had a hardening in my heart. In addition, my pastor also sent me an e-mail stating that my eternal standing was at stake.

I personally believe that God truly ordained marriage, however I don't believe that it is God's nature to exalt the office of marriage above the people that are in the marriage. I believe that the reason that God hates divorce is because of the consequences that occur to the people that are involved in the divorce.

In conclusion, I am in the final stages of divorce and I continue to look to God to direct my family's path and can still say that I have peace in my heart regarding the decision to follow what I believe was and is the Lord's leading. To God be ALL the Glory! He came to set the captives free!

Another woman shared that her husband, who had physically abused her and had been arrested for his offenses, had spent thousands of dollars on a stripper and hidden his financial assets from her had attempted to throw her out of her home with nothing when she asked him to leave. After having consented to 8 weeks of counseling, he insisted that he had done his due diligence. He made it clear to her that, after countless years of abuse, 8 weeks of counseling went above and beyond the call of duty to meet whatever expectations she would dare to have of him. These are not the attitudes of a repentant man who intends to change and love his spouse and family.

Legalism is the refuge of the oppressive, the lazy and the Spiritless.

116

Legalism: The Worship of a Lesser God

...holding to a form of godliness, although they have denied its power... II Timothy 3:5 (partial)

If our Lord's ministry on earth taught us nothing else, we should come away with one thing: The law is not the ultimate answer. Jesus is. The legalist holds to a form of godliness while denying its real power. The law takes precedence while relationship is lost.

Apart from the Spirit, the law can become a terrible taskmaster, words that rise cold and piercing from the page or fall cruelly from a critic's lips.

Yet, Jesus miraculously "dishonored" the law to demonstrate that He was – and is – its Creator and Master. By so placing Himself above the exalted law, at the end of His earthly ministry it was not the dying world that sought to kill Christ, but the highest ranks of learned scholars – the keepers and teachers of the law. They clung to their allegiance to a lesser god, forsaking God's heart for people, for genuine relationship and restoration.

Let us catch a glimpse of the compassionate, relational heart of God as revealed by our Lord Jesus in yet another encounter with the Pharisees.

Then some Pharisees and scribes came to Jesus from Jerusalem and said, "Why do Your disciples break the tradition of the elders? For they do not wash their hands when they eat bread."

He answered and said to them, "Why do you also transgress the commandment of God because of your tradition? For God commanded, saying, 'Honor your father and your mother'; and, 'He who curses father or mother, let him be put to death.' But you say, 'Whoever says to his father or mother, "Whatever profit you might have received from me is a gift to God" – 'then he need not honor his father or mother.' Thus you have made the commandment of God of no effect by your tradition. Hypocrites! Well did Isaiah prophesy about you, saying: 'These people draw near to Me with their mouth, and honor Me with their lips, but their heart is far from Me. And in vain they worship Me, teaching as doctrines the commandments of men.'" Matthew 15:1-9 (New King James Version)

The Pharisees were more concerned with how Jesus and His disciples washed their hands, while looking the other way when those within their circle were neglecting their families' most basic needs – in the name of God.

Jesus saw the depths to which they had fallen and admonished them for closing their eyes and their minds, willingly sacrificing genuine relationship, compassion and grace and instead choosing a perception of piety when their very families were in need. Here we can see the heart of God. Adhering to procedures and elevating the law above relationship is offensive to Him.

In the same encounter our Lord describes a man who, under the law, has clean hands but a treacherous heart. What Jesus describes is consistent with verbal abuse, even referring to cruel speech as murder. Truly verbal abuse is a murder of the human spirit, yet these offenses are so often overlooked or relegated to mere minutiae by many in the Christian realm. Yet, our Lord sees it.

"...the things that proceed out of the mouth come from the heart, and those defile the man. For out of the heart come evil thoughts, murders, adulteries, fornications, thefts, false witness, slanders. These are the things which defile the man; but to eat with unwashed hands does not defile the man." Matthew 15:18-20

How is it that so many in the contemporary church are quick to condemn the Pharisees and fervent in their promotion of a personal relationship with the living Lord, yet just as eager to force believers into the same kinds of legalistic boxes that Jesus so fervently condemned? This is where the contemporary church fails.

The legalists keep us from Christ. Many believers may in time become disillusioned with their faith when it becomes as burdensome as their sin – with the legalists' sword hanging above their heads, while our Lord has sharp words for such as these.

"But woe to you, scribes and Pharisees, hypocrites, because you shut off the kingdom of heaven from people; for you do not enter in yourselves, nor do you allow those who are entering to go in." Matthew 23:13

Conversely, the Scriptures remind us of those things in which God's heart delights.

He has told you, O man, what is good; and what does the Lord require of you but to do justice, to love kindness, and to walk humbly with your God? Micah 6:8

This is the heart of God.

Legalism Kills Compassion

A man was there [at the pool] who had been ill for thirty-eight years. When Jesus saw him lying there, and knew that he had already been a long time in that condition, He said to him, "Do you wish to get well?" The sick man answered Him, "Sir, I have no man to put me into the pool when the water is stirred up, but while I am coming, another steps down before me." Jesus said to him, Get up, pick up your pallet and walk." Immediately the man became well, and picked up his pallet and began to walk. Now it was the Sabbath on that day. So the Jews were saying to the man who was cured, "It is the Sabbath, and it is not permissible for you to carry your pallet." John 5:5-10

Under the law, you're obligated to remain sick. But Jesus says that, in His perfect time, you may be healed. Once again, Jesus' love trumps the law and the legalists stumble, because the gifts of God constitute an inexact science. Jesus colored outside the lines, and He still does. It makes things messy and unpredictable. The legalists didn't like it then, and they don't like it now. But that doesn't change who God is or what He wants to do for us.

In a discussion regarding divorce with one of the pastors of the church we were attending, the pastor asked me if I ever encourage people to get a divorce. I told him 'no,' that I urge people to seek the heart of God.

Then I asked him a similar question: "If a person came to you and said they were considering getting a divorce, would you discourage him or her from doing so?" He immediately responded, "Absolutely. We know that God hates divorce and that marriage is a life-long commitment." I looked him in the eye and said, "That is not your call to make." He was a taken aback by my response – as was I. I urged him to read this book and after he had read it, we met again. This time, he told me early on that the book had changed his perception of divorce, and I asked him, once more, how he might respond to someone who came to him and told him that he or she is considering getting a divorce. This time he replied, "I would urge them to seek the heart of God." He humbly acknowledged that the ultimate answer lies with an individual's personal relationship with our living Lord. I appreciate so much his concession that living under the loving hand of our Lord makes so much more sense.

120

Legalism doesn't allow for miracles, healing or freedom unless it fits neatly into a category the legalists have established. If you aren't doing it according to what the law allows, you're doing it wrong – in fact, it shouldn't be done at all. Legalists will say, *"Your suffering has been ordained by God. Even if you are miserable, at least you're staying safely within the limits of the law and keeping up appearances."* That's the way they prefer it.

So you must choose whether to live according to what the legalists demand and trust that their approval is enough. Or you can follow Jesus and live in the richness of the relationship, power and freedom that God has to offer. You may not be able to have it both ways, though, because some people – perhaps many whom you love and respect - will never understand or approve.

God favors relationship, and relationship is the very foundation of our faith.

"He who is of God hears the words of God; for this reason you do not hear them, because you are not of God." John 8:47

Legalism is Inflexible

So the Jews were saying to the man who was cured, "It is the Sabbath, and it is not permissible for you to carry your pallet." John 5:10

How dare you carry your pallet... The fact that the man was carrying his pallet was evidence of a miracle. He would not have been carrying a pallet if he had not been previously bound to it. Jesus told him to carry it, reminding those who stood by that, if it was more important to observe the law, then the man was better off ill.

When Jesus cast out demons, the same legalists said He could only do so by having an allegiance with Satan. That lines up pretty well with what the legalist church says about believers like me who have been released from treacherous marriage partners. They tell us, "Jesus can't do that," to which I say, "Oh, yes He can."

Perhaps in the arena where marriage is concerned is legalism no more passionately evident. Those who preach freedom in Christ may nevertheless insist that a spouse go home and "fix" his or her marriage even though the marriage partner involved shares not the slightest commitment to do the same. Believers may find themselves cut off from the faith, condemned under the law. End of story. No questions asked. No other option. Our Lord must shake His head as He witnesses such callousness in the name of faith.

One can live for many years seeking to do the will of God against all odds, confident that healing is coming and suddenly find oneself standing in the miraculous grace of God, though bestowed in a manner unexpected and unexplainable. How can it be that such miracles are followed by judgment?

I have almost grown accustomed to the raised-eyebrow inquiries of people who are convinced that my freedom is unbiblical and/or unlawful. When I mention that I was in an abusive marriage for 20 years, the most common response is, "Did he hit you?" When I tell them, 'no,' they look at me with obvious skepticism or abject scorn. Clearly, their presumption is that, as long as my husband was not beating me with his fists, then it wasn't really abuse. These well-meaning individuals – self-appointed judges – have no idea how much pain can be inflicted with a cold stare, a cruel word, undeserved criticism, or demeaning treatment that is constant and deliberate.

Our marriage didn't begin that way. When I met him, the man I married used to spend evenings and weekends down by river encampments or in the poor areas downtown with his best friend, handing out sandwiches and sharing his faith with homeless men. He worked part-time at the church we attended and was a leader in the college ministry. He expressed an interest in ministry or possibly going to the mission field. He was comfortable with children and children loved him. This is the same man who, so many years later, would lock me out of my bedroom as punishment and yell through the door at me to go away, refusing to let me in even to get my bedclothes. This is a man whom I discovered abusing drugs and alcohol, who regularly hid a stockpile of raunchy pornography, and obsessively spent money we didn't have. He would tell me that there was something seriously wrong with me and criticize me either for failing to appeal to him or looking too attractive when I went to work. This is the man who told me that he got along fine with everyone else he knew and that it was just me he despised. When he admitted to dating another woman, he calmly explained to me that he viewed entertaining other women as an acceptable "supplement" to our marriage rather than a conflict and that, as long as I didn't catch him sleeping with anyone, it didn't constitute adultery.

I once saw this man pretend that he was going to beat our two young sons with a belt without cause. Even though I intervened in this cruelty, and we both saw the terror on their faces, he laughed and told me that I was overly sensitive and couldn't take a joke – even while our youngest son wept in my arms. And after we separated, my children told me that when I wasn't home, he would treat them cruelly and threaten them with worse if they ever told me about his actions. This is a man who proudly asserted after our divorce that I wasn't even aware of half of the things he got away with without my knowledge when we were married. I didn't ask...

These are things people like me would never dream of bringing up at church or with a pastor. We're supposed to pretend we're not broken, or maybe just concede that there's no alternative. We're not supposed to hope or believe that God can release us. In some small way, I can relate to the frustration of the blind man who was healed on the Sabbath (John 9). The legalists who would likely not spend a moment to offer me a shoulder to cry on will suddenly view me with suspicion and become obsessed with the legitimacy of my release or restoration! I too should have been free to dance and celebrate my release. Instead I was confused by the church's rigid condemnation.

If He can restore sight to a blind man, He can free people like me who are in bondage to other people, even in marriage. Certainly, He knew the longings of my heart (and the heart of the man who continued to hurt us) and, thankfully, I must conclude that He did not want my children and I to live in bondage for one more day. I have been set free by the only One whose permission or approval I need. It is sad to me that others – so many of my brothers and sisters in the Lord - simply refuse to accept it. But, I and others like me stand in the grace He has given, and I will not waver in it and urge others similarly saved to do the same.

We should no longer consent to the authority of the legalists, for it is they who choose to worship a lesser god.

Defending the indefensible.

The Church: A Sanctuary for the Abusive?

Now I urge you, brethren, keep your eye on those who cause dissensions and hindrances contrary to the teaching which you learned, and turn away from them. For such men are slaves, not of our Lord Christ but of their own appetites; and by their smooth and flattering speech they deceive the hearts of the unsuspecting. Romans 16:17-18

Using what they believe to be their God-given authority, the treacherous find the church to be not only a safe harbor, but a "biblical" defense for their cruel actions against their spouses and children. Sadly, there are those who wield God's word like a weapon to demand unloving, unhealthy and unbiblical forms of submission or manipulation.

"I am the head of this home."
"I make the decisions around here."
"You will submit to me."
"You cannot divorce me."

Even the phrase, "Happy wife, happy life," seems to endow some women with a sense of entitlement that implies, "If you don't give me what I want, I can make your life miserable."

Such are distortions of the word of God and His design for marriage. How wrong it is to extort obedience through heavy-handed demands or manipulation and lay a burden of fear on those who live under the same roof. This is not what God intended. Leadership reflects the wisdom and ability to lead. Godly women will willingly follow a godly leader because the leader's character has been tested and earned. Godly men will want to honor and provide for the woman who respects him.

Submission is voluntary, not under compulsion, but a love offering that grows from mutual trust. In a godly relationship, a husband seeks and values his wife's wisdom and insight, and she ultimately defers to his leadership, because he has proven himself trustworthy. Submission need not be demanded. If a man must arm-twist his wife, something is wrong. A good and wise leader need not demand respect; he commands it.

Yet, spiritual abusers may contort the patriarchal form of family governance the Scriptures support. Male-led homes are certainly biblical in a balanced context where love and respect are central to the relationship. In such homes, there is no overt domination, for it is unnecessary. There is no fear, anxiety, jealousy or competition.

A biblical home is a safe place, not a scary one. No church should provide cover for those who claim marriage as sufficient cause to accept or ignore ongoing sin.

Where is the church that defends the innocent, the church that insists on safety and security for those at risk, the church that confronts the one who continually violates his or her marriage vows? Why is the innocent party expected to maintain a covenant with the one who has broken it? What are the acceptable sanctions and consequences for the individual who has failed to love, honor, respect and protect those within the household? Too often, the innocent are condemned while the guilty find sanctuary, which is utterly inconsistent with God's heart and His design for marriage.

Defending the Indefensible?

"Do not give what is holy to dogs, and do not throw your pearls before swine, or they will trample them under their feet, and turn and tear you to pieces." Matthew 7:6

Some individuals are not worthy of the time it takes to attempt to impart precious gifts of knowledge or wisdom, let alone our precious bodies and loving subservience. These people are vicious and un-teachable and they will use every opportunity to attack those whom they dislike or with whom they disagree.

John Trapp's commentary expounds on the words of Jesus from Matthew 7 (edited for clarity)[6]:

"Having shown how, here our Saviour shows whom we should admonish. Give not holy things, wholesome counsels or rebukes (called elsewhere "reproofs of life," [Proverbs 15:31] precious balms, excellent ointments, which may heal a wound but make none) to dogs, that will not be taken by the ears; or swine, that if they light upon such a pearl, will only grunt and go their ways.

"Beware of dogs, beware of evil workers," (Philippians 3:2), such especially as have wrought so hard, walked so far and so fast, that now they are set down to rest in the seat of the scornful. Beware of such botches; there is no good to be done upon them, or to be gotten by them, but a great deal of danger."

Yet, all too often we concede great deference to the "dogs" that would destroy our families from within, appearing gracious and forgiving (following the official church script) while failing to address the very real destruction of sin in God's sacred institution of marriage. Where is the glory to God when the church boasts in its hypocrisy by choosing bondage over a proper defense of God's marital purpose and design?

Submitting to this church policy of sin-ignorance, there are countless wives (or husbands) who believe that their faithfulness and patience will yield repentance; men or women living in homes where their spouses are irresponsible, cruel or neglectful. The committed spouse strives for peace even while repentance is non-existent. This passivity (enabling) lies to the sinner about his sin and insulates him or her from its natural consequences.

---

[6]John Trapp, Commentary on the Old and New Testaments, (Eureka, CA, Tanski Publications), 1997, online edition

By being compelled to remain silent or accommodate ill treatment, we send the message that habitual sin is acceptable. We affirm it. Allowing the wandering spouse to feel the weight of the consequence of his or sin may (or may not) bring them to repentance. It is a choice they must be given.

And simply standing by and being the "good spouse" does nothing to help the sinning spouse. All it does is allow the "good spouse" to assume the unhelpful status of either moral superiority or martyrdom. Living in a dysfunctional marriage kills family members' sense of their own value, breaks them down emotionally, physically and even spiritually. They become desensitized, confused, heartsick, lonely, and frightened. How can we condone or ignore such disastrous, unbiblical outcomes?

As these unhealthy patterns for relationships and marriage remain un-addressed, they are passed down from generation to generation. While calling these marriages "Christian," the dysfunctional relationships spawn countless ill effects that may include depression, anxiety, eating disorders, promiscuity, drug and alcohol addiction, suicide, rebellion, hostility, rage, and a variety of debilitating health conditions that arise as a result of the stress that children and young people are attempting to live under. The marital charade clearly has the potential to turn disillusioned children away from the faith that could be their salvation – literally and figuratively.

What's wrong with this picture? Everything. We should not be expected to ignore or enable serious moral offenses simply because they occur within the marital relationship. Failing to address habitual sin only serves to perpetuate it.

A man of great anger must bear [his] penalty, for if you rescue him, you will only have to do it again. Proverbs 19:19

Denying the Reach of Evil?

For it is not an enemy who reproaches me, then I could bear it;
nor is it one who hates me who has exalted himself against me,
then I could hide myself from him. But it is you, a man my
equal, my companion and my familiar friend... Psalm 55:12-13

As believers, we live our lives and operate according to a belief
that those who similarly call themselves believers want the same
things we do: relationship grounded in love. It is difficult
enough to admit to oneself that our marriage partner is
intentionally, consistently causing us pain, let alone confess it to
another.

For those on the receiving end of such a confession, when
someone in our circle comes to us and professes fear of their
spouse, parent or other family member, our tendency is to
presume that it is a singular offense. Often we more easily
accept that the offender is struggling and needs our support,
encouragement and understanding to get through what must be a
speed bump, a phase, or a struggle and that the person being
offended against is perhaps overreacting. What we fail to
acknowledge is that there are times when a situation is borne not
of ignorance, but as part of a deliberate agenda to control and
subdue. We are in spiritual denial.

I didn't believe it either – not until so many years had passed,
and it was abundantly clear that my husband was not interested
in being close to me. I was his possession, and he was the
center, not only of our relationship, but the family. What he
wanted, he expected to receive, taking it by force, if necessary.
His needs and desires came first. And, he ruled primarily
through fear and confusion, neither of which are godly traits.

And those who tell victims that we should just pray harder, and
be submissive and loving, have no idea that doing so doesn't
earn the victim any respect; it feeds the oppressor's sense of

power and control. Submission doesn't yield affection, it affirms the opportunity for the self-serving to use a heavier hand and expand his or her power base.

Another woman shares her story.

Katrina's Story

I met my ex when I was in my late teens. I was a young Christian and I met him at a church youth group, but I didn't know him very well. It was a whirlwind romance that moved very quickly, which I now recognize is a red flag in relationships. After a few weeks into the intense relationship, I began to notice a few things that made me feel uncomfortable. He was strong-headed and confrontational in his approach to people and always seemed to have conflicts at work, with church members, and his own family members.

I started to bring up my concerns one night, and he got very sullen, aggressive and intimidating, quoting Scriptures and pressurizing me to stay in the relationship. I had a very deep relationship with the Lord even though I was a young Christian, and felt uncomfortable with the way he seemed to interpret the Bible. But he was so strong in his arguments that I decided to ask our church leaders who knew him quite well what they thought. None of them seemed to share my concern and nobody gave any indication that he would be an abusive life-partner if I went ahead an married him. Since they had known him longer than me, I thought that somehow I must have been judging him wrongly. The warning bells were going off but I had never been trained to listen to the internal warning signals.

I read over 30 books, listened to 20 tapes, spoke to many mature Christian leaders, attended marriage or relationship seminars and not once did I hear anything about abuse in relationships. I was never told of the red flags of violent relationships. All I learnt was that divorce should never be even mentioned or considered, and that the marriage covenant was not only permanent, it was one where even if the other party broke the contract, you could not break it. It was a 100% commitment, meaning that even if the other person gave 0%, you had to be committed to giving 100% of yourself and trust God to meet all your needs.

I tried to break off the relationship a couple of times, but each time, he would vigorously pursue me and hook me with promises. I had never met anyone who gave me that much attention, and I thought it was a sign of true love and commitment. I never quite sensed a Yes or No from God, but in the end, I thought that since most of our arguments were about my lack of commitment, the arguments would cease if we got married, since I knew we would not divorce. I thought we would have a lifetime to sort out our issues and it couldn't be that bad. I didn't have the support of my family because they were far away.

His emotional and sometimes physical violence scared me during our dating relationship, but I didn't see a way out, and he would always turn around and be nice again. I didn't know it was all part of the cycle of domestic violence. We went through pre-marriage counseling, and I tried to express my intense doubts, but did not know how to articulate what the issues were (now I understand that abuse IS the issue when abuse is present). The pastor didn't pull me aside to explore things further, so I took that as a sign that he wasn't concerned.

A few days into our honeymoon, I knew I had made a mistake and cried my eyes out. Knowing that divorce would never be an option, I tried very hard to change myself and make it work. The first few years were filled with abusive incidents, but they settled after the first few years, probably because he knew he didn't have to resort to physical force anymore - I had been trained to jump to his demands. Once he locked me out of the house and I went to a pastor's house. I told the pastor of the physical and verbal assaults, but was told I had to go back to make it work. I spoke to many pastors in the first 5 years of marriage. Many were highly respected counselors but most admitted to me in the end that they couldn't help me. It left me extremely distressed, hopeless and isolated.

After the children arrived, we had a few explosive incidents but they got fewer, leading me to believe that he had changed. It was more of a case that I had learnt to walk on eggshells and became very responsive to his needs and rarely expressed my opinions or stood my ground because I would pay the price for it. But as the children grew, he got more abusive toward them. Being followers of Dobson and well-taught on Christian discipline, we would justify the use of spanking. It disturbed me that he would do it in anger, and I spent many years trying to find ways of solving this problem by reading many books on anger. I tried at different times to bring it up with him, with varying success. Mostly, he would ignore me, clam up, sulk or deny his unacceptable behavioral patterns. Once in a while, he would apologize in tears, making me very hopeful of a change. However, he would never agree to go to counseling.

The only time he agreed to go to counseling was when we had a huge altercation and he wanted me to make an appointment with a recommended marriage counselor because I needed fixing. I thought this would be the turning point. This Christian couple listened to him, then listened to my very cautious revealing of how he violently attacked me and threw things at me. To my surprise, the man said that he understood how my husband felt and asked if I was controlling. That really threw me and I began to wonder. They also said that I needed to open up more and that communication was about being emotionally open. So instead of protecting myself, I exposed myself to him even more. The sessions stopped after I was told to change my behavior and my husband got what he wanted.

As the children became teens, our fights became less but his fights with them increased. I spent a lot of my energy trying to solve this for him and for them. I suggested counseling to him, but he stormed out and slammed the door after a few angry words. I began to share with another pastor, hoping to get others involved. My husband hated me disagreeing with him in front of the kids, which I had to if he was raging at the kids, so I

135

tried to talk to him behind closed doors. That wouldn't work either because he would storm out of our room and yell at the child in question, accusing the child of driving a wedge between us. After a few years of escalated abuse and almost unbearable tension in the home, this pastor said he would try to talk to my husband. He came around a few times and tried to give him counsel, even visiting regularly and challenging him with Scripture. However, without intensive work on abusive attitudes, nothing changed.

Finally, one day, the Lord spoke to me and showed me that I was being loyal to a person walking in unrighteousness. I knew it was true - I was too scared to stand up to him. If he had glared at me and insisted I walked with him through the gates of hell, I would have felt obliged to follow. I also a got a few dreams about how my life would go into upheaval, and that the family would break down. One day, the Lord intervened. He got arrested for physical abuse of a child. The pastor had told me not to report the incident, so I didn't. That didn't stop him from accusing me of turning him in, something that he felt was the ultimate act of betrayal from a wife. His abuse escalated. My pastor told me that that was the time to speak up. I did, resulting in more abuse. His abuse became more and more psychological.

I still sought support from the pastor, who suggested we go away by ourselves. That thought terrified me, and fortunately it didn't happen. My husband reluctantly went to see a recommended Christian psychologist, who also asked to speak to me, then to both of us together. He told me that I had failed to bring up the kids in a godly way, that I should not have reported the assault (even though I hadn't), that I shouldn't have told anybody about it but my husband, that I should have always presented a united front to the kids, even though I had rarely ever disagreed in front of the kids. This psychologist maintained that ours was a mutual problem. After a few months of seeing him, I asked him about separation, and he insisted that separation never worked. He

136

said that there was no option but to stay together and work it out. He didn't even agree that I had the right to walk away if he got verbally abusive during a conversation.

At the same time, I started to see a recommended Christian counselor from our church. When my husband found out, he insisted on coming as well. He used the joint sessions to verbally abuse me, and there was nothing the counselor could do. He would complain about me, and she would turn to me to say that I was contributing by rolling my eyes. She also supported him by saying that our children were perpetrators of domestic violence by throwing things in frustration. I eventually asked if I could see her separately, but she was not keen because she thought saving the marriage was the priority. She also said that I had to put the marriage above the children, even when it was obvious that the children were being mistreated and were showing signs of trauma. She would not recommend separation either.

One day, I was at the end of my tether, and cried out to the Lord. The devotional reading for the day was about the Exodus of the children of Israel. The Lord told me that I should just walk through the Red Sea. I didn't see how it would happen. I called up a domestic violence crisis service and booked a spot in a shelter, but felt that Isaiah 52:12 "You shall not go out with haste, or by flight" would apply to me. I felt the green light to go, but was waiting for the right time to speak with him. At the same time, a trusted confidante got a prophetess to speak to me. This prophetess, who only knew that I was intending to separate, said that God would turn everything around if I stuck around. She said that things would get worse before they got better, but I needed to try harder, pray more and be gentle and not challenge my husband. She also added that if I did separate, everything would go bad, he would panic, withhold the finances, and that the children would hold everything against me, warning me that this was what the Holy Spirit was saying, which was more important than what any pastor or counselor would tell me. I

137

was so paralyzed by this word that I spoke to another pastor, who fortunately warned me against believing any personal prophecy hook, line and sinker.

My husband also got a few allies of his to talk to me and they asked me how much I valued my marriage, and that I ought to support him more because he was suffering with the tension of the court case. They didn't seem to appreciate how much my children were suffering. My children even asked me why adults were more concerned with protecting another adult than looking after the safety of vulnerable children. I had no answer for that.

After his court case was over (during which he got a light penalty), things didn't get better. Not long after that, I told him that I was wanting a separation. He started crying and promised that God would change him. He also offered to speak with pastors, friends, and do anything to save the marriage. I stuck to my guns and within a few days, he left. It happened just as God had promised - a smooth journey through the Red Sea. Since then it has been an up and down journey as his post-separation violence and harassment continues insidiously. It has been very difficult getting support from Christians, especially because of his smear campaigns. From being an uncommitted believer, he has become very active, joining a few Bible Study groups, attending prayer meetings and offering his help in other ways. He has also managed to pull many leaders and some unsuspecting pastors into colluding with his abuse by making them pass messages to us or stalk us. He certainly doesn't present as a perpetrator of domestic violence, and has managed to isolate me by drawing many people to his side, in spite of the fact that I was a very active member and he wasn't.

Fortunately, God has sent a handful of supportive Christians into my path. Mostly, they are either survivors of abuse themselves or professionals in the domestic violence sector. My other supporters are secular advocates. What my former Christian friends and his current allies don't understand is that

God is more interested in the restoration of human souls than in preserving an institution. They also don't understand that they will not get a picture of the truth by listening to him, since abusers are manipulative. They don't understand that there is a cycle, and that remorse is not repentance. They don't understand that just because he cries or says he knows he needs to change doesn't mean that he has changed or that he will be safe for us to live with. "Improving" or "being nice" is not change. They also believe wrongly that forgiveness means that I must be on friendly terms with him. They don't understand that abuse is not a mutual relationship issue. Mostly, although they understand that it is not God's will to be in an abusive marriage, they don't recognize abuse when it stares them in the face. I was assessed as being in high risk domestic violence, and I had never once heard about domestic violence during all the 25 years that I sought counsel from church leaders.

Sometimes we heap hot coals on the wrong heads.

Unintended Consequences

Further Hurting Hurting People

I'll admit that my pastoral experience soured me to opening up to others in church about my marital pain. Clearly, I figured I could expect a typical Christian-ese response, but no real measure of genuine understanding, compassion, encouragement or support. When I was compelled to separate from my husband, I immediately stepped down from the worship team on which I was serving. The music pastor I served under, whom I had known for years, offered his sympathies but didn't have a real idea what to do or say to me. He wished me well. That was more than I could hope for. At least he didn't condemn me.

But, these many years later, having survived an abusive marriage and begun a ministry to women in similarly abusive relationships, I have been stunned at times by the judgmental behaviors of pastors and church people toward women who are not merely struggling but suffering on a regular basis.

One woman who wrote to me shared that she went to seek counsel and help from her pastor after leaving her abusive husband. He listened to her account, expressed his concern, escorted her out of his office and, as she walked away he reminded her, "Remember, God hates divorce." She was no longer sharing her burden; the full weight of it had been returned to her shoulders. She left her husband and eventually divorced him just the same, with a clear conscience and a sense of peace she never doubted. At this writing, her abuser is still harassing her. Many in her church have condemned her for having a hardened heart because she sought freedom from her husband's treachery, with no word of correction toward her spouse who had been emotionally bludgeoning her into submission.

When I asked another dear friend of mine what her experience was when she was being abused, she said this: "The church didn't know what to do with me. We were both serving in ministry. I told friends what was happening in my home, how he was treating me. They told me to be more quiet and submissive. And the quieter I became, the meaner he got. It didn't end until he left me for another woman."

Remember "Gwen," whose story was told earlier in the book? Here is her account of an encounter with men at her church many months after her separation:

I did brave up one evening after church and spoke with the man who is our interim preacher right now, since our former preacher changed churches, and also two of the men who are deacons or elders at our church. One evening I decided I had enough of his slander and bad talk about me and my children. I just could not take it anymore, and that night after church, it was fairly quiet and those three men were standing in the foyer, and I asked to speak to them.

I told them that I wanted them to hear my side. That I was tired of nobody knowing my side and how I felt, and that I wanted to keep quiet about the situation but Frank would not keep quiet and kept slandering and talking badly about me, and I felt pushed to tell them my side of things.

I even played for them my voice messages in which Frank tells me to get out, threatens me financially, shows his control and etc... I absolutely poured my heart out and cried many tears. Even after all of that, the interim preacher still tells me that he would fight for the marriage and told me that he felt I was trying to 'justify' my divorce, and then told me that there was only two reasons for a marriage to separate that were okay with God. And these were death and infidelity. I believe that one of the men had compassion for me, and I could see it in his face. He did not encourage me to stay in the marriage. The other man did. So two out of three said I should fight for my marriage, go to counseling and try to work it out.

I will tell you, though, that I stood my ground. I told them that I felt like God was okay with my marriage ending. I told them this was what my children wanted also, and that we are all happier now. I even told them how my children felt, how both of my sons told me at different times how the song "Open Wounds" reminded me of their dad. Nothing changed their mind. But, I told them that at this point nobody could pay me enough to go back in that home and live with that man again. That felt good. I went up against them and stood my ground.

I cannot say that I really expected to get support from them. I believe I shared that with you, that I was hesitant to go forward because of the fear of rejection. And I am glad that I did wait until several months had passed and I had gained some strength before I went and spoke with them. If this had been earlier in the separation, I believe it would have hurt me and defeated me more, but given as I am so sure of myself, and sure of my relationship with God, sure that this is what He wants me to do, that I did not let their opinions sway me.

Before I left they all three prayed, and I want to be honest with you, I know that the two of them were praying about keeping the marriage together and healing hearts, but I am sorry if this offends you, I only half-heartedly listened to them. I do not want their prayers to keep this marriage together. This marriage is over. And it has been terribly broken and beyond repair for many years.

I know that what these men see is black and white. They aren't seeing the shades of gray that are so obviously there. I wish these men would read some of the books that I have read. I wish they would open their eyes.

I contemplated a great deal for many reasons leaving the church and going elsewhere. Somewhere that Frank had not infected people with his lies and his fake goodness and all around false self. But, after giving it some thought I have decided, at least for the time being, not to change churches and for this reason. I have a 15-year old son and 11-year old son that want to go to church. I don't know that many 15-year old boys who want to attend church. I believe this is the time in their lives where they want to stop going to church and etc... but my son wants to go. And if I am sick or my daughter is sick and I cannot go, he will get a ride with one of his friends so he doesn't miss church. After weighing that in my mind, I decided I will stick it out there and the main reason is that one.

I know the truth. I know what happened. I know I gave it my all. I know I gave it every single chance that I could. And I know that me being free from him is exactly what God wants for me. I know because I weighed and prayed about it for such a very long time before I left, and therefore I stand firm in my faith.

These men do not know what happened in my house. They don't know that I gave it my all, in fact I know that Frank has told everyone quite the opposite. And he is still trying to get me to come back to him, as we speak. And sadly enough, Christian people keep encouraging him to keep the marriage together. They don't realize he is stalking me and harassing me. They keep telling him not to give up on the marriage and his family, and it makes me sick. Because they are only feeding his obsession. But, again I do realize these people are only seeing black and white and nothing else.

...So many in the church need to know the truth. They need their eyes opened."

I am proud of Gwen for speaking her truth, based on *her* relationship with God. She was not asking for those men to

146

release her; she was simply asking them to acknowledge that she had been released.

They didn't. But, Gwen continues to press on, strong in the assurance that the Lord is her protector, her advocate, her friend and merciful judge.

Trite Answers for Troubled Relationships

Most Christians come biblically equipped with a collection of three-second sound bites that enable them to keep a safe distance from a suffering individual while giving the appearance of faith and support. These are some of the morsels that roll off many a believer's tongue:

"Count it all joy, when you encounter various trials..." (James 1:2)

"Rejoice always, again I say rejoice." I Thessalonians 5:16

"God causes all things to work together for good for those who love God..." (Romans 8:28)

"Love never fails..." (I Corinthians 13:8)

"Pray without ceasing..." (I Thessalonians 5:17)

"Seventy times seven..." Matthew 18:21-22

"Be anxious for nothing, but in everything by prayer and supplication with thanksgiving, let your requests be made known to God, and the peace of God that passes all comprehension shall guard your hearts and your minds in Christ Jesus." Philippians 4:6-7

This is the kind of religious, empty talk that trivializes the heartache of living in a destructive relationship – and even legitimizes it. A man or woman seeking intercession, affirmation of his or her experience, and help may instead find little acceptance or even acknowledgement, only another measure of guilt, expectation and ignorance heaped upon him or her.

The hurting partner has probably exhausted every possible means of trying to get his or her spouse to care. The church may be quick to embrace the drunkard, the homeless, the prostitute, the drug addict, or the gang member, but too often there is some awkward discomfort associated with the separated or divorced.

As believers, we feel a strange, even arrogant obligation to assess and judge for ourselves whether the divorce was necessary and biblical (from our own way of thinking) and who was at fault. Our faith is inherently questioned. If only our faith was strong enough, we wouldn't find ourselves in such a pitiable position.

Dear friends, the time has come for the walls to come down, for the secrets to be told, for our arms to be extended to those who are suffering untold terrors in their own homes. We need to be willing to call sin what it is and tend the wounds husbands and fathers and wives and mothers are inflicting on those they are called to love and protect. The church doesn't even know the kinds of horror it defends.

It was the evening before Thanksgiving, and a night I will never forget. I had approached my husband to discuss some issues relative to his drug and alcohol abuse, over-spending and poor treatment of me and our children. As the discussion continued, he began a verbal assault that I felt inadequate to combat. He cleverly rationalized that every shortcoming on his part was a result of a failure on mine. He was so passionate and long-winded that by the time he had finished with me, I felt I had nowhere to turn. Even though I could not see the truth in his words, they were true to him, so either he was telling me the

148

truth, or he was deliberately trying to hurt me. I couldn't bear to believe that.

So, I finally broke down, accepted his account and tearfully confessed that I was a lousy wife. He was delighted. He had me. He then told me that he felt it was my obligation to tell our children what all of the fuss was about. I begged him not to put me to such shame and humiliation, but he insisted. He called our four children into the family room and asked them all to sit down. I could not help but weep, and the children (all under the age of 10) began to cry. My husband told them that I had something to say. And, I shamefully told them that the troubles we were having were my fault; that I was a lousy wife. And our children came to me and hugged me as I wept. It had to be one of the most horrible moments in my life. I knew in my heart it was a lie.

My husband sent the children to bed and insisted that I have sex with him even while I wept. He loved it. He was victorious. He had completely broken me and got what he wanted – total domination over me. If only I had had the strength to say 'no.' I felt I had to prove that I was not a lousy wife. What he did was terribly wrong and cruel. Even all these years later, it still hurts.

My husband never struck me – at least not with his fists. But time after time, month after month, year after year, he attacked me where it hurts most. I had scars alright, but none anyone could see, and open wounds that took years for the Lord's light and affirmation to heal. His grace is sufficient, yet the scars remain.

Many have been led to believe that abuse must be physical. It is precisely this long-accepted, well-circulated falsehood that keeps abuse victims in bondage. Unfortunately, there are still pastors, lay people and believing friends who defend such prehistoric logic.

The Terrible Stigma of Divorce

An overseer, then, must be above reproach, the husband of one wife, temperate, prudent, respectable, hospitable, able to teach, not addicted to wine or pugnacious, but gentle, peaceable, free from the love of money. I Timothy 3:2-3

This Scripture has been misappropriated as an edict that insists that divorced people are disqualified from ministry. Churches often teach that *the husband of one wife...* means that the candidate for ministry has been married only once, therefore, a divorce and/or remarriage requires the automatic disqualification from service in public ministry.

Commentaries make it clear that the actual issue to which Paul is alluding is polygamy, consistent with the practice of "putting away." Keeping multiple wives was acceptable within the culture but unacceptable in the body of Christ. Yet, many church bodies continue to use this Scripture to exclude divorced people from ministry. There is nothing in Scripture that makes any such assertion, nor any similar disqualification from service for the believer whose love for the Lord is evidenced in their walk with Him.

No other segment of believers is ever ostracized so. Divorced people often feel like outcasts within the church. The Apostle Paul could have been discredited as a result of his background as a persecutor of the church, yet he became a pillar of the New Testament church.

If anything, I am more adequate to minister than at any time before in my Christian life. There are no secrets. There is no shame. My marriage to my husband is as strong as any I have ever witnessed. We are viewed as a couple whose marriage exemplifies the very best in biblical relationships, and with good reason. God has continually affirmed and blessed our union.

150

Others easily perceive the intimacy and balance that characterizes our relationship. Yet, the validity or potential value of what we have to offer may be called into question by our past. This stigma seems to be reserved only for the divorced – in fact, the abuser who knows how to play his cards right may be an elder or a deacon, while his wife may expect to be condemned should she leave him. Others have been not only ostracized but formally excommunicated for leaving or divorcing an abusive spouse.

A dear friend of mine shared with me how her father abandoned her mother and their four children who were then between the ages of 2 and 8. This was in the 1960's. Following the divorce, the woman moved with her four children into a small duplex and did her best to provide for them as she tried to fit in with the community. One day my friend's mother shared her grief that, although she had tried to make friends with the women in the community, her efforts were rejected. She wasn't sure if the married women feared that she would try to steal their husbands or if her status as a divorcee was a black mark on her general reputation. Either way, she felt like an outcast, and she had done nothing wrong. How sad.

God does not hate divorced people, nor does He relegate them to second-class status. God does not abandon the abandoned; why would the church?

In Matthew 12:11-12, Jesus reminds the religious, *"What man is there among you who has a sheep, and if it falls into a pit on the Sabbath, will he not take hold of it and lift it out? How much more valuable then is a man than a sheep!"*

The Sabbath is the single most important ritual observance in the Jewish religion and culture. It was described as the bride, the queen. Yet, Jesus openly defied the legalists by demonstrating His preference for another bride – His people.

151

When abuse occurs in *this* church, will victims receive help in their time of need?

We urge you, brethren, admonish the unruly, encourage the fainthearted, help the weak, be patient with everyone.
I Thessalonians 5:14

There are no secrets.

Soul-Searching

The Heart of The Matter

As in water face reflects face, so the heart of man reflects man.
Proverbs 27:19

God sees what is unseen.

It is such a strange phenomenon: getting old. As I have aged, and the laugh lines and wrinkles become more apparent, it is obvious that whatever outer beauty I may have possessed in younger days is fading. On the other hand, as the years have passed, even while my outward appearance slowly fades, I have become a far more joyful, contented and secure woman. I tell my friends with a wink and a smile, "Aging is God's way of reminding us that we need to be beautiful on the inside." While we may be tempted to measure ourselves based upon appearances, such assessments are ridiculously flawed and foolish. How we appear is an inaccurate measure of who we are.

God makes it clear that it is not the external that matters to Him, but that which emanates from within. It is there that convictions are cemented, grudges are nursed, evil is plotted, and wounds fester. And it is in the heart that love smolders into flame and courage is stirred, and from it goodness pours forth and forgiveness flows.

God sees it all. He perceives the intricacies of our motives, longings, priorities and passions. He knows what drives us, tempts us and touches our hearts.

He knows who we are.

But the Lord said to Samuel, "Do not look at his appearance or at the height of his stature, because I have rejected him; for God

155

*sees not as man sees, for man looks at the outward appearance, but **the Lord looks at the heart**."* I Samuel 16:7

God is not fooled, nor is He impressed. The holy, all-knowing, eternal Creator-King of the Universe is uninterested in the title printed on our business cards, the sum stashed in our bank accounts, or how many friends we boast on Facebook™.

As prone as we may be to be influenced or deceived by appearances, God cannot be. God is imminently aware of our heart's condition.

For the eyes of the Lord move to and fro throughout the earth that He may strongly support those whose heart is completely His. II Chronicles 16:9

The God who created us sees all that our heart contains. The secret resentments, any ill will or selfish objectives we harbor are plainly visible, exposed and uncovered before the Holy One.

We may find ourselves convinced by smooth talk and an easy smile. There are those who offer up prayers, stand shamelessly in the limelight, speak with authority and grace, or rub shoulders with those in places of influence, believing that they are well concealed. But, it is the Lord who judges rightly, the One who sees all that is hidden.

Woe to those who call evil good, and good evil; who substitute darkness for light and light for darkness; who substitute bitter for sweet and sweet for bitter! Woe to those who are wise in their own eyes and clever in their own sight! Woe to those who are heroes in drinking wine and valiant men in mixing strong drink, who justify the wicked for a bribe, and take away the rights of the ones who are in the right! Therefore, as a tongue of fire consumes stubble and dry grass collapses into the flame, so their root will become like rot and their blossom blow away as dust; for they have rejected the law of the Lord of hosts and despised the word of the Holy One of Israel. Isaiah 5:20-24

It is He who takes account of those whose heart is His, who live in the light of His love. It is He who steadies the weak and upholds the righteous. It is He who rewards our faith.

The righteous man will be glad in the Lord and will take refuge in Him; and all the upright in heart will glory. Psalm 64:10

The Heart Reveals Motives

The plans of the heart belong to man, but the answer of the tongue is from the Lord. All the ways of a man are clean in his own sight, but the Lord weighs the motives. Proverbs 16:1-2

If we try hard enough and look long enough, we can justify almost anything in our own heart and mind. The drug addict believes the lie, "I can stop whenever I want to," the pornography addict tells himself or herself, "I'm not hurting anyone," and the abuser says, "She deserved it." God knows when we are saying one thing to a friend's face and quite another behind his or her back.

Regardless of how we may justify our actions or the lies we tell ourselves – and choose to believe – the Lord knows our motives. He knows when we are being self-serving and when we are acting out of genuine love, respect, hospitality or compassion.

If there are times when I feel closed off from God, it may be that my heart has been hardened by the self-centered belief system I have adopted, and the poor choices that belief system has yielded. When I put myself first, then God is not first. My heart betrays me. As each of us searches our own heart, as we open our heart to Him and ask Him to reveal our wicked intentions, we can then seek forgiveness and ask God to work in us to change our ways.

157

Motives are tricky things. Do they arise from the subtle voices that our minds entertain? What do we want, and how do we intend to go about getting it? It is not so much about what we do, but *why* we do what we do.

In acknowledging the constant battle between our flesh and the Spirit, motives are not always evaluated before we move forward. But, as we allow the Lord to search our hearts, the Spirit prods us and empowers us to act according to His will and not our own.

Why would I ask Him to speak to me
if I do not wish to hear what He says?

Living By The Spirit

The Holy Spirit: Our Intercessor

Righteous are You, O Lord, that I would plead my case with You; indeed I would discuss matters of justice with You: Why has the way of the wicked prospered? Why are all those who deal in treachery at ease? You have planted them, they have also taken root; they grow, they have even produced fruit. You are near to their lips but far from their mind. But You know me, O Lord; You see me; and You examine my heart's attitude toward You. Jeremiah 12:1-3a

We can plead our case before the Almighty. When we are lost, alone and afraid, we know we have an advocate in Him. He hears the cry of our hearts and knows our plight. He is our defender and guide and comforter.

We stand before the Lord in humility, seeking mercy and divine provision. He makes a way.

He intercedes, provides a way of escape, meets the needs of our hearts, and lights the path before us. Sometimes all we can see is the one step before us, and it is enough. He is personal and powerful and aware when we call upon Him. At times it can feel scary or risky, yet His will will be done. It may not feel perfect, but He will use it all, He will make it so.

That's what a life of faith looks like. It may not be what I expect or what I ask for. It will be what is best.

Conviction and Peace: Guardians of the Heart

Search me, O God, and know my heart; try me and know my anxious thoughts; and see if there be any hurtful way in me, and lead me in the everlasting way. Psalm 139:23-24

The decisions you make regarding your relationship are between you and God alone, which requires soul-searching and self-examination. By allowing God full access to your heart, He will begin to reveal to those things in your life that need to be acknowledged, offered up, changed, and/or forgiven.

As you seek to follow the leadings of the Holy Spirit in your life, God provides two essential guardians by which your heart will be governed: conviction and peace. In any given situation, you can generally expect to have one or the other.

It all begins with a humble plea that the Lord would examine our heart, expose every corner, every careless or doubting thought. Then we ask God to show us areas where we need work. And finally, we ask Him to lead us in the "everlasting" way, to enable us to live in a manner that has eternal value. His way is the way to contentment and inner peace.

Yes, there are times when the Spirit prompts – a gentle nudge when each of us knows that He is calling upon us to do something - or do nothing; speak - or remain silent. And when the moment comes when we have responded to His calling, and our hearts are free of conviction, then there is peace; God's perfect peace. It is an excellent balance of correction and affirmation. In embracing and being compelled by these guardians of our hearts, there is a rich freedom, for it is not our will we seek, but His.

In relationship with Him, the beauty is in actively, faithfully and sometimes painfully responding to His promptings that come from conviction. For each one of us, it may mean acknowledging a failing or changing an attitude or behavior. Once it is acknowledged and offered up to Him for His correction or forgiveness, or when we act according to His leading, peace will follow. And when we find ourselves listening for His voice and release is granted, God's perfect peace accompanies it.

In my case, my divorce process seemed to languish on unnecessarily, and many of my friends advised me as to how I should hurry things along, push my attorney, and close the book. But when I sought the Lord in prayer for His counsel, I sensed His conviction strongly upon my spirit, *"Wait."* Every bone in my body wanted to fight it, and there were times I prayed for a different answer, tried to convince myself that forcing things along was the best solution, but I could not escape the gentle prodding upon my heart.

"Wait. Just wait." Doing nothing, knowing I was risking everything, was perhaps one of the most difficult things I have ever done. But, when closure finally came, I was able to see clearly how God's hand of protection was at work in the perfect timing of it all – for my protection and that of my children. I am so thankful that I listened to His voice above all others. It was a difficult lesson, and one I will never forget. And juxtaposed against His call on my life to wait, when I least expected it, He released me!

As He has guided me in the days, months and years since, I have strived to listen and respond. I haven't always succeeded and have had to repent of my selfishness or stubbornness time and again. But He knows my heart, and I have come to fully appreciate the freedom that comes from surrendering my will - that far exceeds any pleasure I find when I serve myself. The peace of God I enjoy is worth having and well worth the wait. It is a rich reward indeed.

Joy is the end result, because as I respond to His promptings and follow His lead, I know that a path has been laid out for me; a path that leads to intimacy with my Lord and that glorious peace. Abundant life. Just what He promised.

Be anxious for nothing, but in everything by prayer and supplication with thanksgiving let your requests be made known to God. And the peace of God, which surpasses all comprehension, will guard your hearts and your minds in Christ Jesus. Philippians 4:6-7

My eldest daughter shared with me about a Christian woman she knew who had decided to divorce her husband, and when she inquired further of her, the woman told her that she just didn't feel like she wanted to be married anymore.

She questioned me about the legitimacy of this woman's decision. I cannot answer for her. That is between her and God. But, I can say that if the woman had asked me for my advice prior to her divorce, I would have urged her to petition the Lord to search her heart, to be receptive to any conviction He placed upon her spirit, and to act only when she had peace.

That's the way it's supposed to be. Conviction belongs to Him, and so does the peace that comes from responding to it.

Frequently Asked Questions

What About Forgiveness?

Then Peter came and said to Him, "Lord, how often shall my brother sin against me and I forgive him? Up to seven times?"

Jesus said to him, "I do not say to you, up to seven times, but up to seventy times seven. Matthew 18:21-22

Question: How many times must we forgive someone who has harmed us?

Answer: The same number of times that we are harmed.

But wait. The answer is often misconstrued in Christian circles. Many fail to teach clearly what forgiveness is – and what it isn't. We are called to forgive for one reason and one reason only as the encounter in the eighteenth chapter of the Gospel of Matthew points out: because we ourselves have been forgiven a lifetime of sin. The debt we owe and could never repay has been paid in full.

As a secondary benefit, we forgive, not for the sake of the offender, but to free ourselves from the eventual root of bitterness that grows out of harbored resentment. We release ourselves from the need to carry the burden of anger that eats away at our spirits and our daily lives. We release that burden to God and let Him carry it and do with it what He wishes and to impose a penalty on the offender, if any, according to His will.

Never take your own revenge, beloved, but leave room for the wrath of God, for it is written, "VENGEANCE IS MINE, I WILL REPAY," says the Lord. Romans 12:19

Yet while forgiveness basically releases an offender from any consequences his or her victim may be inclined to impose, forgiveness does not release an offender from other natural or divine consequences. Natural consequences are those that are a consistent and logical result of the offense. If a man beats his wife and is arrested, not only will he suffer under the due process of the legal system, he may spend a pretty penny on attorneys' fees, time in court and perhaps in jail. He may also rightfully forfeit the companionship of his wife and the trust of his children, his family, friends and co-workers. It may be that restoring those relationships requires genuine repentance and perhaps many months or years spent re-earning the trust that was lost. Some of those relationships may be permanently forfeited. Those are natural consequences.

There may also be divine consequences. This truth is seen time and time again in the Scriptures. Our Lord is extremely forbearing and patient. Yet when God's people continually rejected God's standards and His law, He removed His hand of protection and saw His chosen people wander for years in the desert, taken into captivity or die in bloody battles. After David took Bathsheba and discovered that she was carrying his child, David had her husband killed in an effort to hide his sin. David and Bathsheba's first son died as a measure of God's divine judgment.

Thirdly, releasing an individual from any restitution or revenge does not constitute an agreement that the relationship is restored. Forgiveness is not a commitment to pretend that the offense was never committed nor should we ever expect that, once mercy is bestowed, the individual committing the offense is somehow automatically welcomed back into our circle of trust. That is an illogical presumption that sends godly people back into unsafe relationships with potentially evil people. Just as our Lord commanded His disciples to be "as shrewd as serpents and as innocent as doves," so are we to walk in wisdom and discernment of the Lord in our daily lives. The biblical mercy of forgiveness was never intended to make us foolish.

Nor does an apology equate to repentance. We do not find the Scriptures urging us to apologize. An apology may be offered for any number of reasons. The one apologizing may say, "I'm sorry you are hurting," rather than saying, "I'm sorry that I hurt you." There is a huge difference between the two. The one apologizing may also confess to hurting you but add a condition, "…but, if you hadn't…" That is not an apology; it is a rationalization for the inappropriate behavior. There is no "but" in a sincere apology. Whatever the case, an apology need never be assumed to reflect genuine repentance, nor does repentance invoke the need for reconciliation.

What About Separation?

It is strange that many within the church readily accept separation (which is *not* biblical), while refusing to accept divorce (which *is* biblical).

There is nothing in the Scriptures that urge marital partners to separate in an effort to address marital distress or failure. Separation may have merit for many couples who need time and distance to work through various logistical issues, heal from wounds inflicted, and assess whether the couple can be reconciled. That makes perfect sense. However, if eventual reconciliation is deemed mandatory, then the unrepentant partner need only bide his or her time and say the right things, knowing that obligation will compel reconciliation even if nothing in a darkened heart has changed.

Yes, common sense supports the validity of separation, but it should not be presumed that separation will ultimately result in restoration. This is not an issue to be decided by the marriage partners and the pastor or the church; it is an issue to be decided by each believer as he or she seeks the heart of God.

What About Vindication?

O Lord, You have heard the desire of the humble; You will strengthen their heart, You will incline Your ear to vindicate the orphan and the oppressed, so that man who is of the earth will no longer cause terror. Psalm 10: 17-18

In affliction, the Lord is our rescuer and defender, even in marriage. Churches tend to teach that our God can surely rescue us from virtually every form of trouble or evil – except perhaps an evil marriage partner.

At one point I discovered that my husband had entered into a dating relationship with another woman shortly after I had given birth to our third child. (This was not his first lapse of sound moral judgment, nor would it be the last.)

The morning following the revelation, I awoke after a fitful night's sleep and decided to go into work early. Riding a commuter train that was virtually empty, I felt almost paralyzed by the depth of the heartache. Crushed and feeling numb, I sat bleary-eyed on the bench, staring out the window as the sun began to glow a faint orange above the skyline while the tears fell uncontrollably. I made not the slightest utterance, but could do nothing to stem the unrelenting wave of grief and sorrow. In the lonely silence, I whispered in my heart to God. "I can't trust him, Lord." And, instantly, I heard that unmistakable, inaudible voice say, "But, you can trust Me."

In that moment, my relationship with my husband and my relationship with my Lord changed. I could not see it then, but I see it now. No longer was I simply my husband's wife, under his authority. I was my Father's daughter brought under His wing of divine protection and provision. His tender voice gave me the courage and resolve to press on. I knew I was not alone. "Okay," I said in my spirit. "It's You and me, then."

I wasn't giving up on my marriage. I was giving it over to the One to whom my vows were made. I would put Him first, seek His heart, and follow His leading. And, to the best of my ability I did.

Eight long years later my husband and I separated, and almost ten years after that terrible day, we were divorced. And, my Father, my Defender has been with me every step of the way. Did I plan on divorcing my husband? No. Did God affirm, comfort and provide a way for me when I did? Yes.

The Scriptures are replete with God's receptiveness to the cries of the afflicted, to free them, and to condemn and turn back the proud and the unrighteous.

Indeed, the Lord was and is my strength and my shield. He validated me as He has validated others. I will not be ashamed.

...Jehovah is my rock, and my fortress, and my deliverer, even mine; God, my rock, in Him will I take refuge; my shield, and the horn of my salvation, my high tower, and my refuge; my savior, you save me from violence. II Samuel 22:2-3 (1901 American Standard Version)

What About The Children?

[Blog post dated July 9, 2012. This is an important subject to address when it comes to the complexities of divorce and, for this reason, I choose to reprint it here.]

"It is better to be from a broken home than to live in one."

I wish I knew the name of the pastor I heard on the radio who offered up that stunning statement. I'll admit my surprise knowing it was a pastor who said it. I remember smiling to myself and exclaiming aloud, "Thank you." For what he shared is something rarely heard.

For an abuse victim who dares to reveal to her friends and family members her inclination to leave her abuser, she often hears something quite different than what the pastor asserted. She will more likely hear, "What about the children?"

There it is: an emotional trump card, a ticking time bomb. Any convictions about escaping the emotional harm she and her children might face on a daily basis are at once upended and she finds herself catapulted into visions of an unavoidably disastrous future. Could it be that perhaps separating from the abuser will only make things worse? Is it true that a child is better off in an abusive household where both parents are present than in a broken home?

Today, a full decade after signing off on my divorce decree, I have to say from my experience that the pastor's sentiment makes perfect sense. Having seen both sides, being from a broken home is far superior to living in one. I also recognize that some will contest that statement and insist that a life of separate households and the blow of a severed marital relationship are somehow more destructive. That is someone else's story to tell. This is mine.

When I finally left with our four children, the kids were between the ages of 6 and 13. My relationship with my husband had deteriorated to such a state that I was on the verge of a nervous breakdown. The five of us lived in a constant state of fear, and the children struggled with various degrees of depression, anxiety and anger, which was most evident in the two eldest. I had done what I thought was right to maintain some semblance of normalcy, stand up for the kids when I caught my husband being overly harsh with them, deflect his anger to myself, and try to create a "happy" home. The abuse had increased so incrementally over time that I had a hard time seeing the magnitude of the dysfunction, the massive weight of oppression under which we strived to survive. *Maybe tomorrow things will be different,* I used to think. *Maybe tomorrow he'll care.* Tomorrow never came. All of my good intentions failed. Our lives never improved; in fact, they became increasingly worse.

Looking back, I can see how each child responded uniquely to the abuse, the separation and our recovery based upon their ages, personalities, perceptions and history. We have all had to work hard to reclaim our value and rebuild our lives individually and as a family. The life we share now is healthy and safe, nothing even remotely like the hell we were living in before we left. There were several things I was able to do for my children to help them get from that place of brokenness to a place of emotional health and stability.

First: I had to admit to the harm.
In most cases, while trying to live in an abusive relationship, our tendency is to overlook, minimize or blatantly deny the abuse. We rationalize that our abuser's actions are simply consistent with male or fatherly behavior. We remind our children that their father really loves them or attempt to diminish their anguish by using pathetic excuses like, *"He doesn't mean it,"* or *"He's just going through a hard time right now."* What we are really saying is that our children's feelings are not as important as their father's right to treat them badly.

Once we finally break out and acknowledge to ourselves the depth of the harm that has been done, it is vital to affirm the truth to our kids; not to burden them with our stories (which should not be borne by them), but to acknowledge theirs.

The night my kids and I left, we hurriedly packed up our most vital possessions and loaded up my van. I came out with a last armful to see the kids all sitting in their seats in silence, tears streaming down every child's face. So, I stopped everything, and we went inside and sat down together to discuss the answer to the unspoken question: What was happening to our family? After explaining briefly why we had to leave, I asked them what was going on with them. One by one, they timidly began to share their own experiences, things that had happened in my absence, terrible words that had been said, secrets they were expected to keep. As each child shared, they all became empowered to speak up. After they finished, I simply said to them, "I am so sorry. That is abuse, and it's wrong. We are not going to live that way anymore." The words absolutely seemed like too-little-too-late, but on the other hand, I suppose it was more akin to better-late-than-never. The admission was critical, and I saw in their eyes an immediate response, visible evidence of hope.

Second: Give them a voice.
The dance of dysfunction continued for many more months, even after John moved out and the kids and I moved home. John's hide-the-ball attempts to address his addictions, abuse and his wandering eye failed, largely because my children were now empowered to share their experiences with me. They began to tell all, and when they talked, I listened, and they appreciated that I took their complaints seriously. Even my youngest daughter, only 6 at the time, didn't hesitate to say, "Mommy, I need to talk to you about something." It gave the children value and the freedom to identify actions and situations that they knew were clearly inappropriate.

It meant a lot of confrontation between their dad and I, and he hated that his coerciveness had been exposed, but now the kids and I were all working together to acknowledge the truth and speak the truth so that I could better confront it. I got all of the kids into counseling, so that they could also speak to someone objective about their experiences and even share their disappointments about me as their mother, which they had every right to work through. In many ways, I had absolutely failed

172

them. Whatever was necessary to achieve their healing and restore their sense of their own value; I wanted them to have it.

One woman who was trying to escape an abusive marriage told me how her teenage daughter was acting out and doing poorly in school, and the woman just wanted her daughter to knock it off, and she asked me if I had any suggestions. I asked my friend if she had spent any time with her daughter to find out what was going on in her daughter's life, knowing that perhaps her daughter was struggling with what was going on at home. My friend looked at me like I was from another planet and dismissed my question completely. I fear the poor girl is simply begging, by her actions, to be seen and heard. Unfortunately, it seems that her mother simply doesn't want to be bothered.

Third: Help them to feel secure and loved.
I always wanted them to feel safe at home, but that whole dynamic had been obliterated by the abuse. For example, on Saturday mornings, the kids and I would get up before their dad and have a great time eating cereal, sitting in the family room together and watching cartoons. When we would hear his footsteps on the stairs, I think a tremor of anxiety ran through us all, and we would go silent. Sure enough, upon descending, John would begin barking orders to the kids and tell us to turn over the remote, because we had had enough fun, and it was his turn to watch what he wanted.

I never wanted them to feel that way again. We had to rebuild and reclaim what we had lost.

Although I worked full-time, I arranged an adjusted schedule so that I could get home earlier to have more of an evening with them – to converse over dinner, help with homework or be available to talk. I basically cleared my calendar. Other than lunch with friends from work or going out for coffee occasionally, my very purposeful intent was to restore their sense of security by being available to hug, help and hear them –

to remind them daily for as long as necessary that I wasn't going anywhere. It was time and energy well-spent.

I have heard of some parents who, upon separating, immediately move into the singles scene, or live their lives as though nothing traumatic has occurred. The children are left in a state of constant doubt as to what is going to happen to them and whether the custodial parent also intends to leave. And we wonder why they become depressed or anxious or sick or end up on drugs or alcohol or become promiscuous or end up with an eating disorder. They simply need to know they are secure and loved. If you have the opportunity to give that to them, please make every effort to do so.

Fourth: Walk toward a new and better life.
We talked about our future. We all knew where we had come from. Now we needed to decide where we were going. In the end, what we wanted was a healthy, happy family where everyone felt safe, respected, accepted and supported. We had Friday family movie night and watched Disney movies and ate pizza and microwave popcorn and laughed and sang along with the songs. We went out of town on vacation, if only for a couple of days, just to rediscover what it meant to drive a long distance and listen to whatever music we wanted to hear on the radio, to not live by one person's schedule, to really relax without pressure or drama or guilt. All those simple things were so healing. My kids were free to claim and live a life that they all wanted. And I wanted that for them.

It has been a long, winding, rough road chock full of pitfalls and imperfection and struggles. The children still smart and grieve from many of the wounds they carry that were inflicted when their father lived with us – and since. But what we have accomplished together, and the healing and faith and strength and wisdom and character and growth in my kids' lives in the past ten years have been worth defending, worth striving for.

174

So, what about the children? That question caused me to doubt my instincts and live in fear of the future for too long. In hindsight, seeing what my children endured, I have far more guilt for the years we stayed than for the years since we left. In truth, once we left, we stopped living a lie and embraced the truth: It is far better to be from a broken home than to live in one.

But He knows the way I take; when He has tried me,
I shall come forth as gold. Job 23:10

Conclusion: God Is My Witness

And this is another thing you do: you cover the altar of the Lord with tears, with weeping and with groaning, because He no longer regards the offering or accepts it with favor from your hand. Yet you say, 'For what reason?' **Because the Lord has been a witness** *between you and the wife of your youth, against whom you have dealt treacherously, though she is your companion and your wife by covenant.* Malachi 2:13-14 (emphasis added)

God lays an indictment at the feet of the Israelites with regard to the treachery they had committed against their wives. In John Gill's Commentary regarding verse 14, he states:

"...when espoused together in their youthful days, the Lord was present at that solemn contract, and saw the obligations they were laid under to each other, and he was called upon by both parties to be a witness of the same; and at the present time he was a witness how agreeably the wives of the Israelites had behaved towards their husbands, and how treacherously they [the husbands]had acted towards them; he saw and knew, that, whatever pretensions they made, they did not love them, nor behave as they should towards them; and therefore had just cause of complaint against them, and must be a witness for the one, and against the other..."[7]

There it is...*a witness for one and against the other...*

At one point during my separation from my husband, I called a prominent, pro-family ministry and was put in contact with a Christian counselor. She graciously spent some time with me on the phone, and I explained what I had been living under and asked for her counsel. I gave her a brief chronology consistent

---

[7]John Gill, John Gill's Exposition of the Old and New Testament, (London, Mathews and Leigh), 1810, online edition.

with what I shared in this book. She listened patiently and then asked me one question: Why are you still with him?

I'll admit my shock at her frankness. I had prayed for him, submitted to him, kept his secrets, had every possible conversation with him to encourage responsibility and restoration, and seen multiple marriage counselors. No one had ever given me permission to even leave, let alone divorce him.

Neither did counselors ever mention abuse to me, although looking back it was glaringly obvious. As silly as it seems, initially I had no understanding that it was possible to be abused if my husband wasn't hitting me. It was certainly never discussed in church. Not until I stumbled on a book about verbal abuse was I jolted into a sobering reality regarding the gravity of my living situation. In spite of the insanity of our lifestyle, I had been committed to the typical church-approved response, although I finally realized it was not the biblical response.

A biblical response would have included the church leadership accepting testimony and seeking an audience with the errant spouse to demand confession and repentance. If that intervention failed, then the victim could procure the testimony of two or three witnesses, clearly identify and condemn the immorality in the relationship, support and encourage the people or persons who were put in harm's way, and expect repentance from the stubborn spouse. But, from my experience, it is difficult to discover whether this biblical approach is ever utilized.

Upon disclosing the nature of our collapsing marriage, none of my believing friends recommended seeking support from my church body. I think they sensed, as I do now, that the church would have done little to assist me and, in fact, might have encouraged me to continue being "faithful" by remaining in the relationship in spite of the negative impacts doing so would have on my children and me. How sad to think that the church might be the last place a married man or woman in legitimate pain should be encouraged to go to ask for emotional and spiritual support.

In spite of the telephone counselor's inquiry, I did not pursue divorce at that time. Even though separated, I did have hope.

Months later, the moment came when the Lord released me. I have never been more certain of anything in my life. I have heard the tender, inaudible voice of the Holy Spirit at other times in my life, but not this time. It was more like an indelible impression, a movement upon my spirit. I was not in prayer nor was I in crisis. Yet, God was there.

I was having a telephone conversation with my husband. He lied to me, and I knew it. And, when the realization of what his words hit me, it happened – a moment filled with perfect clarity and affirmation. It felt as though a tremendous burden was being lifted from my shoulders, the weight of pain, sorrow and longing for my marriage was removed and, though there were no words, the impression I sensed in that precious moment was, *"You have fulfilled your obligation."*

I calmly told my husband, "That was it." When he asked me what I meant, I told him that it was over, and I would be filing for divorce. I felt no anger or hostility, no fear of regret – only absolute peace.

I have never had a moment's doubt about God's affirmation, nor have I once regretted my decision to divorce my husband. The God who had accepted our union did not sever it; my husband did. And, it was God who granted me a divorce, not my husband, not the courts, not my pastor, and not the church. It was God who was my witness. It was He who led me through that dark valley, He who began to heal my heart, He who protected me and my children. It was He who made a way when there seemed to be no way.

181

Nevertheless, even since, I have had many well-meaning, believing friends assert that what I did was a sin and that, having remarried, under the strictest interpretation of Scripture, I am committing adultery. .

But God is my witness. Jesus makes it clear that the hardness of men's hearts affords a legitimate need for divorce. The Holy Spirit is alive and working in my life, and He has the authority within the very real, personal relationship that I enjoy with Him to release me – and He did. My marriage relationship had been adulterated. For years I had been neglected and abused by one who had also made vows to love, honor, cherish, protect and provide for our children and me. My former husband stood on the law to shield himself from the consequences of sin, while God calls us to stand on love as His higher law and allow the natural consequences of sin to fall.

As He released me, can He not also do so for others?

Because I love marriage, because I believe that marriage is meant to serve as a wondrous, earthly example of the loving relationship between Christ and the church, divorce is intended to protect those who would otherwise be left unprotected and to defend and uphold the integrity of God's sacred bond.

I believe that we as a body have a responsibility to elevate godly marriages and emulate them. We have a responsibility to allow the light to shine on selfish and sinful behaviors for the purpose of reclaiming marriages. This is not to openly shame individuals, but to call to repentance those who claim the name of Christ while blatantly violating God's intent for marriage.

We have a responsibility to come alongside those whose marriages have been torn asunder by those within the relationship. We need to open our arms and our hearts to those who have kept the terrible secrets, uphold them in prayer and encourage them to seek the Lord's will in their relationships, rather than the church's.

This also seems counterintuitive, but if the permissive nature of divorce was more readily understood, it could create a valid mechanism to encourage moral renewal rather than simply settling for mediocre and tepid marriages. While the unbending commitment to marriage has the potential to urge partners to stay in unhealthy or dysfunctional marriages no matter the cost; conversely, recognizing the potential threat of losing one's spouse, family and home could spawn an insurgence of repentance and genuine commitment to the oneness that marriage is meant to reflect.

Malachi 2 confirms the willingness of God Himself to advocate on behalf of the offended. In this instance, the Father stands in the gap against men who had failed their brides. Malachi's exhortation is obviously designed to rebuke those who had dealt treacherously with their wives – those who had made solemn commitments but had not kept them. The same Father still advocates on behalf of men and women who have been betrayed, neglected, abused or abandoned.

So then, because of His love for the honorable intentions of marriage, the Father is not only willing to express His disapproval, but to command repentance. Yet, the body of Christ, it seems, is often loath to do so. In an ongoing effort to adhere to an essentially politically correct understanding that elevates the office of marriage above its sanctity, the church becomes an enabler, a co-dependent, that props up marriages that are not simply unhealthy, but destructive, in an effort to offer the appearance of holiness, whether in marriage or in the church. It seeks to keep those who live in the midst of treachery and bondage in it regardless of the costs or terrible outcomes that the churches' directives may incur. With the kindest of intentions and no malice of forethought, it is a result of a design to accept simplistic theology rather than perceiving the larger picture and God's higher law.

And all the while the world is looking for authenticity. It is looking for genuineness where it may be found. So many churches endeavor to cover a dead marriage with flowers of so-called faith to attempt to repress the stench, although the design to protect itself rather than the beauty of marriage ultimately reeks of hypocrisy.

Keeping spouses in harmful, hurtful, broken marriages for the sake of marriage does not change the fact that the marriages are still harmful, hurtful or broken. This is a call for repentance to those who take the marriage state lightly, flout its sanctity, ignore its responsibilities and use their partners for selfish gain or accommodation.

Again, this is a mutual commitment that must be adhered to fully and completely (if imperfectly) or the one-flesh bond will not exist. Some marriage partners wish to gain the upper hand in the relationship. They look out for their own interests and exploit or manipulate their marriage partner, often knowing how to play the game to get what they want without humbly recognizing or honoring God at the center and truly loving his or her spouse.

If only a small percentage of godly marriages were, in fact, evidencing the genuine intent for marriage, their example would be far more valuable and exemplary in the eyes of the believing and unbelieving community, knowing that those who honor their vows are those to whom we should look as examples of what marriage should truly be.

Ignoring or rationalizing the maintenance of unhealthy, even destructive, marriages that inflict pain and shame upon the entire family and the church is foolishness. For those who are committed to not just remaining married but *being* married, grace and healing are available. Nevertheless, there are those who demand an adherence to marriage, not for the sake of marriage, but for the sake of appearances. Our Lord clearly frowns on such hypocrisy. Why do we condone it?

Now when He had spoken, a Pharisee asked Him to have lunch with him; and He went in, and reclined at the table. When the Pharisee saw it, he was surprised that He had not first ceremonially washed before the meal. But the Lord said to him, "Now you Pharisees clean the outside of the cup and of the platter; but inside of you, you are full of robbery and wickedness. Luke 11:37-39

God is my witness. And He is a witness to those who are being told that they must remain in cruel or destructive marriages. God does not condone treachery. Such sins within and against the body must be acknowledged and addressed.

If God is my witness, I need no other.

Even now, behold, my witness is in heaven, and my advocate is on high. Job 16:19

Statistics and Stories

...my enemy will say, "I have overcome him," and my adversaries will rejoice when I am shaken. But I have trusted in Your lovingkindness; my heart shall rejoice in Your salvation. Psalm 13:4-5

Although free under God, I am at times condemned by my brethren. I am a hash-mark on the wrong side of the Christian ledger.

Statistics are an imperfect measure, and certainly fail to capture the true nature of relationship. As a born-again Christian, it always pains me to hear quoted the percentages of those who call themselves believers who have been divorced. We must

185

conclude that many within the body have failed to live up to God's given directives. Surely, this burden of sheer numbers compels us to count and recount the cost before adding to our collective failure.

But, brokenness cannot be measured in such stark terms; it occurs one person at a time. God is not seated before His heavenly calculator tallying up the casualties. We know His heart breaks, recognizing that a hardness of heart is the catalyst that predicates divorce. Nevertheless, each of us is seen as an individual child in His eyes, not a number.

Before the destruction of Sodom and Gomorrah, He promised Abraham that He would withhold His hand of destruction if Abraham could identify a faithful remnant. God knew full well that the people's hearts were cold and hard, but He wanted Abraham to acknowledge the justice in His act and see for himself the depth of self-abasement to which people can fall.

So Abraham dug deeper, looking into the eyes of individuals for signs of grace, and tragically concluded that only Lot and his family merited saving. In the midst of harsh, righteous judgment, so we still see God sparing the one who was faithful, the one who knew better than to look back.

Statistics are not mere numbers. They represent real people with unique lives and circumstances that cannot be measured with simple calculations. Each marriage destroyed is heartbreaking. Some divorces are unnecessary and regrettable, borne of selfish or sensual desires, and others are relationships that have been "put asunder," torn apart by one partner or the other or both. As we have seen, God offers a stern warning to those who tear apart what God has put together. But this is not to say that it does not happen, and ignoring this may result in all within the broken circle living a destructive lie.

God did not see me as a statistic - someone who would make Him look bad. He saw my imperfect heart, a sincere faith, and my longing to see our marriage and family saved. He also saw my former husband's increasingly selfish motives and poor choices that ultimately tore our marriage to pieces.

It seemed improbable that through my divorce, God would bless. He has brought me a wonderful husband although I wondered if I would ever be able to accept or give love again. My children and I have enjoyed a deep, rich spiritual and emotional healing that was unattainable while our abuser lived in our home. And, no longer consumed with fear and a struggle to merely survive, we are free to empathize with others in similar circumstances and help them to see that God sends His goodness and grace (in whatever form it takes) when we are faithful.

If you must see me as only a statistic, please put me on the right side of the right ledger. I am a divorcee. But, beyond that, I have been redeemed by the blood of the Lamb; I am a follower and friend of the Most High God. My name is written in the Book of Life. And, in the end, that's the only measure that really matters.

Each of us must choose what, or whom, to believe.

What We Should Have Been Taught

The Lord is near to the brokenhearted and saves those who are crushed in spirit. Psalm 34:18

The Lord is an advocate for the weary and the oppressed, and the initiator of the love relationship we are called to enjoy with Him and with others.

Relationship is Paramount

It is love that propelled Heaven's Son to respond to the desperation of our plight, to save us from the eternal damnation that awaited us. In Him, our relationship with the Father is restored. Jesus is the Lord of the law and the only One who could fulfill it. The law points us to God, for the law cannot save us – we are only condemned by it. With redemption, the Holy Spirit was provided as a gift to accompany us and speak to us in our daily lives.

Marriage is Sacred

Marriage was designed by God to serve as an earthly example of the mutually loving relationship between Christ and His bride, the church. The relationship is to be governed and compelled by love. There is a beautiful balance between the One who gave His very life for His beloved to save her, and the bride who submits to and serves the One who lavishes her with love and relishes relationship.

This marital union is to be held in highest honor and esteem. God sees not only our actions, but the motives by which we are governed. There are no heart attitudes or choices that are unseen by Him.

Vows Matter

It takes two people to establish a strong marital bond, but only one to break it. That which has been broken or violated may be restored; however, only when there is genuine repentance can the bond be saved. And, because marriage is sacred, in the event that one party in a marital relationship acts from a hardened heart or is unwilling to repent and change his or her ways, divorce is provided as a means of providing release to the man or woman who has been emotionally, physically or spiritually abandoned. Men and women who remain in adulterated relationships continue the cycle and the curse of dysfunction that many families live under.

Divorce is Biblical

Shallow missives such as "God hates divorce," misrepresent God's heart to those in failing marriages. Destructive marriages do not serve Him, His children, His people or the lost well. God is offended and does not approve of those who would trample upon His beautiful design and the wondrous example He has set.

Divorce represents an admission that there has been a refusal by one party or another, or both, to adhere to His will and His ways. However, divorce it not a sin unless the heart is wrong. It is a public acknowledgement that a marriage bond has been broken by sin. Divorce was provided to protect those who are otherwise unprotected, honor those who have been dishonored, and free those who would otherwise be held in bondage in violation of God's design.

Sin Should Not Be Accommodated

The law of love emphasizes the appropriateness of acknowledging blatant abuse or neglect that may occur in marriage, the motives of the marriage partners, each one's divine accountability to God, as well as the personal witness and promptings of the Holy Spirit. There are some who clearly exploit the law, as well as the convictions and nature of their victims to keep them in bondage. The Scriptures make it clear that such derision should be identified and addressed.

The open toleration of sin will ultimately permeate and harm both the marriage institution and the church, which should serve as God's most favorable example. It is foolishness to turn a blind eye to sin in defense of marriage.

The Spirit Leads

The Holy Spirit is our law and our guide. As He weighs our hearts and our motives, we have a responsibility to listen to and obey the prompting we receive from the Holy Spirit, to stand on the truth, and to serve Him with a clean heart and from a pure conscience.

It is not the church's role to rule or judge those who are striving to walk in Him but to come alongside and encourage those who have endured undue suffering in marriage, to understand that discipline is appropriate for those who shun correction or live in sin, and to uphold the sanctity of the marriage institution. For those who admit that their marriage is painful or failing, we can offer a hand of comfort, a word of encouragement, a prayer for restoration. But, rather than judge or bind those who are hurting, there are three primary exhortations that should form the essence of our response.

- Search your heart. *...be diligent to be found by Him in peace, spotless and blameless...* II Peter 3:14 (partial)

- Pray for wisdom. *But if any of you lacks wisdom, let him ask of God, who gives to all generously and without reproach, and it will be given to him.* James 1:5

- Listen for and respond to the voice of the Holy Spirit. *But I say, walk by the Spirit, and you will not carry out the desire of the flesh.* Galatians 5:16

There is no doubt that it is relationship God loves and for relationship He came. Even now, the Bridegroom is preparing to receive His bride, the church. He is her Savior, the lover of her soul. A wedding feast is planned in honor of the Lamb, He who rides the white horse of victory, He who holds the Book of Life, the One worthy to open the seals of judgment.

Conversely, we confess that earthly marriage is the union of two flawed people who, ideally, are striving to serve and love one another with humility and affection. The deceiver knows that marriage is designed to inspire us to see the picture of Christ and the church in its earthly display of unity. The destruction of marriage and family brings heartache and disillusionment, with the enemy's ultimate goal being to keep us from God.

As believers, we can point others to God – to strengthen marriages and contribute to the oneness the Lord loves and the world needs.

Restoration is possible if both marriage partners make it plausible. Nevertheless, with God as my witness, for the sake of marriage, in order to uphold and honor truth and righteousness, the Lord most graciously intercedes.

"...I am He who knows and am a witness," declares the Lord. Jeremiah 29:23b

Some blessings from God will nevertheless be condemned.

Accepting an Unpopular Gift

The issue of divorce is not the most pleasant of subjects. However, as I have so often shared, I am a grateful recipient of the grace and power of God to redeem and bless a life that I thought might be beyond recovery. I can well recall walking under a dark cloud of desperation for days or months at a time. There were times I wondered whether my prayerful petitions were fruitless. Yet, deep down I knew that my Lord had not forgotten nor forsaken me. I knew that He would, in His time, make a way.

He did.

During the long years I prayed and waited, struggling to live with the chronic pain, I convinced myself that I expected too much or that my suffering was a direct result of my inadequacy as a wife. There were many lies I believed that were surely bolstered by an incomplete understanding of God's love for marriage and for me.

Once released, I was nevertheless ashamed of my failure, my history, and my label. I had always held to a strong conviction to never accept divorce. As a child of a broken home, I knew well the trauma that divorce brought with it and was convinced that I would never take such a path.

So, in the process of walking through separation and divorce myself, seeing the fear for the future in the eyes of my children, it was made worse by those who shunned me. Others subtly or even openly rebuked me for my disobedience or "in a spirit of Christian love" flatly branded me an adulteress in accordance with their narrow view of the Scriptures.

I clung to the Lord and His gift rather than well-meaning know-it-alls, not even certain why He chose to set me free. But now I know.

Since those days I have seen His hand of provision, restoration and affirmation. Now that I have been restored, I delight in sharing how things have turned out for me and my family, to remind myself of how far we have come, but also to acknowledge the path God has so wondrously laid out before us.

More than a year after my divorce was final and several years of ongoing counsel, I cautiously reentered the dating world. I did not consider myself a prize, but more closely akin to damaged goods. As a woman in my 40s, still working through some of my wounds and raising four children between the ages of 8 and 15, most men who initially conveyed an interest quickly backed away when they discovered the parental responsibilities that still lay ahead. And most of those who were interested in me didn't interest me. So it wasn't long before I was thoroughly disillusioned with the notion of dating, and I was prepared to accept and remain satisfied with the peace and contentment I was enjoying as a single mother.

Just before my online Christian dating subscription was to expire, a gentleman new to the site initiated contact with me. After two weeks of e-mails and phone calls where we shared the depths of our history, the foundations of our faith and our dreams for the future, our relationship seemed to be headed in a very favorable direction.

Living 400 miles apart, and both of us smarting from our unique emotional wounds, we were equally cautious. Once we were finally able to meet and spend some time together, it became apparent that we what we enjoyed was precisely what each of us was seeking. Doug, having 2 grown sons of his own, didn't see my young children as a burden, but rather as an opportunity to bless and lead and minister to them.

Three short months after we met, he left behind his life, sold his home and accepted a transfer to my neck of the woods, and four months after the move, we were married. I've heard of people who "just knew," but I honestly never believed that such a thing was possible. And since our meeting, these two formerly divorced people have seen our lives, and the lives of my children, his children, and many with whom we associate blessed by our love for one another, our faith and our ministry.

We have all healed greatly from the treacherous wounds we carried, though the scars are still there to remind us of where we've been and how far we've come. And all of the credit and glory goes to the God who loves us and intervened.

I see myself as a happily married woman, not as a formerly divorced one. I have watched our ministry grow and am continually amazed to meet and come to know so many men and women who have been set free by the truth and power of God. I stand with those who have chosen to listen to one small voice above all others.

With immeasurable gratitude I can boldly say, "Behold, He makes all things new."

* * *

---

[i] Walter L. Callison, Divorce: A Gift of God's Love (Leawood, KS, Leathers Publishing, 2002)

[ii] Transcript of Saddleback Teaching on Abuse, http://dannimoss.wordpress.com/for-clergy/articles-for-clergy/transcript-of-saddleback-abuse-audio-clip/, Accessed Internet June 9, 2011

[iii] Transcript of Saddleback Teaching on Divorce, http://dannimoss.wordpress.com/for-clergy/articles-for-clergy/transcript-of-saddleback-church-teaching-on-divorce/, Accessed Internet June 9, 2011.

Other Books by Cindy Burrell

Why Is He So Mean to Me?

Divorce God's Way

Everything My Heart Seeks

More articles and resources are available at
www.hurtbylove.com.

Made in the USA
Lexington, KY
15 March 2015